DIS

1991

SAVING OUR ANCIENT FORESTS

SETH ZUCKERMAN

THE WILDERNESS SOCIETY

LIVING PLANET
P R E S S

Los Angeles

*This book is dedicated to family, friends,
colleagues, teachers and all the people who
walked with me in the forest.*

—S.Z.

Interior design and page layout: Merlin Clarke
Cover design: William Whitehead
Cover illustration: Mercedes McDonald
Interior illustration: J. Wiley Bower
Printing and binding: R. R. Donnelley and Sons Co.
ISBN 0-9626072-9-0

> To order additional copies of this book, please use the
> order form on the last page or look in your local
> bookstore. Discounts are available for bulk orders.

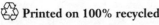 **Printed on 100% recycled Crosspoint Sycamore paper**

Manufactured in the United States of America

Library of Congress catalog card number 90-064447

CONTENTS

PREFACE

Think of it this way: The remaining ancient forests of North America survive in a narrow band stretching from southeast Alaska through British Columbia, Washington and Oregon to northwestern California. Together, these forests add up to enough territory to make up a good-sized nation. If you were told that this imaginary nation was systematically ripping up virtually all of its ancient Sitka spruce, hemlock, Douglas fir and western red cedar – along with all the life forms that depend on these magnificent trees – you probably would be appalled. How could such a country survive, you might ask, if it plays havoc with its most precious natural resource? The answer is that it could not hope to survive.

The ancient forests of North America are not those of a single nation bent on pillaging itself, but they are being brought to the verge of extinction just as relentlessly. Ninety percent of our trees – 300 to 900 years old – have been cut, and the 10 percent that remains is all we will ever have. For generations now, these forests have been devastated with such single-minded purpose that it will take nothing short of congressional action to save the little that is left. Many individuals and groups are working on the passage of an Ancient Forest Protection Act that intelligently addresses the issues of biological diversity, preservation of the vanishing old-growth forests, and the future economy of a region that finally is approaching the inevitable end of the long road of careless exploitation.

I urge you to support the efforts of The Wilderness Society and other conservation organizations in their efforts to keep this magnificent legacy from oblivion. If you doubt the urgency or importance of the task, this splendid book should enlighten your mind and inspire your concern.

—Senator Gaylord Nelson
Founder of Earth Day

A JOURNEY THROUGH TIME

A JOURNEY THROUGH TIME

To walk into an ancient forest is to step back in time. Tens of millions of years ago, dinosaurs roamed through groves of giant conifers, ancestors to the trees that now grow on the west coast of North America. Through the eons, the trees evolved into the species we see today, while the jostling of the earth's crustal plates raised the mountains beneath them. Over the last 100,000 years, different trees have been displaced by changing climate, spreading ice sheets and competing plants. Occasionally, stands of trees were killed by erupting volcanoes, windstorms or fire. But despite these natural upheavals, large communities of virgin forest survived.

About 10,000 years ago, the glacial ice melted and the climate warmed. Gradually, forests spread out to blanket much of the North American continent. Today that blanket is in shreds. Only small, scattered fragments of ancient forest remain. The best examples are now located along a strip of land running from Northern California to the Alaska Panhandle, from the

Pacific coast inland one or two hundred miles to the crest of the Sierra Nevada and east of the Cascade mountains. Here you will still find pristine forests of cedar, Douglas fir, Sitka spruce, ponderosa pine and hemlock that have been growing for thousands of years – so long that we call them "ancient."

Imagine yourself in such a forest. Let your eyes sweep from the foot of a tree up its broad trunk to the lower branches several stories above. Even higher up, through a scatter of limbs and distant needles, you can barely make out the treetop and, beyond it, small patches of blue sky. Like other visitors to the forest, you may compare it to a cathedral. The towering trees seem to swallow sound as you move deeper into the sheltering grove, the faint echoes of your footsteps punctuated by an occasional birdcall or small animal scurrying through the underbrush. The air is rich and fragrant, as it is after a rainfall.

Around you, the spaces between the trees are filled with waist-high ferns, some of the earliest plants to appear on earth. The forest is a palette of greens and browns, dappled with occasional bright orange spots of fungus. As you walk, the ground feels spongy under your feet, padded with a thick layer of needles and twigs. In front of you, a huge fallen log, almost as tall as you are, blocks your path.

Suddenly the harsh revving of a chainsaw startles you. The noise continues for about 10 minutes, then stops. You can just make out a shout, "Down the hill!" then a cracking sound, growing louder and louder. The cracking is followed by a whoosh of branches sweeping through the air and brushing against nearby trees and limbs. Finally, with a great crashing and shaking of the earth, a huge tree plunges to the ground several hundred feet away. The chainsaw starts up again and the logger begins to divide the tree, which was already a mature 200-foot-tall specimen when the Pilgrims landed at Plymouth Rock. In the time it will take you to read this book, hundreds of magnificent old trees like this one will fall to the chainsaw in the forests of the Pacific Northwest.

The forests are threatened

From the fjords of Alaska's Inside Passage to the rugged hills of the Sierra Nevada, ancient forests face the threat of severe logging. Forests that have existed for thousands of years are falling before the saw at an alarming rate to be processed into lumber, plywood and paper. It's no mystery why the forests are being cleared; they contain some of the finest timber on the planet. In the areas that have been logged most heavily – Northern California, Oregon and Washington – close to 90 percent of the Pacific coastal forests have already been cut, and the pressure is increasing to fell the last of these forests. In Alaska, 40 percent of the richest forests have been cut. In British Columbia, 60 percent of the coastal stands are gone, and the remainder are falling at a pace of 100,000 acres per year. At current rates of cutting, conservationists estimate that most of the remaining ancient forests which are not protected from logging will be entirely gone in less than 20 years. Even some in the timber industry have admitted that these forests will not last beyond the middle of the next century.

The old-growth forests of the Pacific Northwest – and those east of the Cascade mountains, as well – are a unique legacy, a magnificent product of millions of years of evolution. Yet we humans are destroying them just as we are beginning to learn about the astounding variety of plant and animal life they harbor, as well as how the forest helps to maintain topsoil, filter the water that runs through it and moderate the earth's climate.

The trees of these ancient forests are more productive than those of any other forest outside the tropics, and incredibly complex relationships have developed between the plants and animals that live among them. It is precisely this intricate diversity of life that makes these forests so special. The ancient forest is home to the marbled murrelet, a bird that spends most of its life at sea but depends on old-growth forests to make its nest in beds of moss and lichens on the branches of ancient trees. The forest floor provides a safe haven for salamanders that rely on the moisture and coolness of decaying logs to survive the heat of summer. Here are the essential fungi that help trees draw nourishment from the soil and flying squirrels that spread the spores of the fungi to other trees in the forest.

Despite everything scientists have discovered in the last 25 to 30 years about the ancient forests, much remains a mystery. Each fresh finding is a reminder of how much we have yet to learn. Trying to fathom all the intricate links among the inhabitants of the forest is a humbling process. It's daunting to think that we are destroying something we don't yet fully comprehend.

Changing our ways

In Northern California, Oregon, Washington, British Columbia and Alaska, nearly 200,000 acres of ancient forests are cleared every year. That's almost 500 football fields per day. These ancient forests are irreplaceable. Once they are gone, and when the species that depend on them have vanished, there is no way to bring them back. We must, therefore, preserve the ancient groves that remain, develop other ways of obtaining the timber our society uses and find ways to use less wood.

Society may always call upon some of the Pacific Coast forests to satisfy its need for shelter and fiber. The issue is: How can we protect the integrity of the ancient forest ecosystem and still meet those needs? Even from the standpoint of timber production, ancient forests are critically important. The untouched wild forests hold the key to understanding what a healthy forest requires from us.

The timber industry has used up nearly all the old-growth forests on the lands it owns, and wants to do the same on the public lands as well. Most of the remaining ancient forests in the United States are controlled by two federal agencies: the U.S. Forest Service and the Bureau of Land Management. In Canada, the public forests are governed by the Province of

British Columbia. These agencies manage the forests on our behalf. That means that all of us as citizens share the responsibility for how the forests are treated.

This book tells the story of these forests so that we who care about them can speak up for the values that are ignored in the headlong rush for more timber and timber profits. We must protect what remains of these dwindling forests to preserve the diversity of plant and animal life on the planet, as well as for the clean water, cleaner air and the scientific, recreational and educational benefits the forest provides. Our challenge is to do this while, at the same time, planning for a sustainable livelihood for the people in the region, as well as a supply of timber. But we must put the forest first to protect the quality of life for ourselves and for future generations. This book will show you how.

THE INCREDIBLE
ANCIENT FORESTS

THE INCREDIBLE ANCIENT FORESTS

An ecology of unique systems

The ancient forests are the most tightly packed communities of living things anywhere on the planet. A single acre of ancient forest contains nearly 400 tons of wood in the tree trunks alone, not even counting the leaves, twigs, branches and roots. These forests contain the most massive living things on earth and hold more commercial timber per acre than any other temperate forests.

The ancient forests, in their many variations, stretch along the Pacific Coast for thousands of miles. Imagine an osprey on its annual migration back from a winter in Mexico. First it flies over the ancient forests in California's Sierra Nevada, where firs, pines and cedars grow in the mixed conifer forest. Scattered here in small groves are the giant sequoias, the largest living things on earth – some of them more than 3,000 years old. Veering westward, then north along the coastal fog belt, the osprey soars over the redwood forests, home to the tallest trees in the world, at least one towering 367 feet high. As the bird continues north, it crosses through the mixed evergreen forest in the Klamath and Siskiyou mountains on the California-Oregon border. Here are the most diverse conifer forests in the world, including sugar pine, Port-Orford cedar, incense cedar, Pacific yew and Douglas fir. Interspersed with these are broadleaf trees, such as tanoak, Oregon oak and madrone. On the mountain slopes, the forest blends gradually into a northern version of the mixed conifer forest, and higher still, into the subalpine forest of the high country.

Continuing toward its summer breeding grounds, the osprey passes over the Douglas-fir forest, the classic woods of

EASTSIDE STORY

The forest doesn't stop at the summit of the Cascade mountains but changes on the east side of the ridge, where the "eastside forests" begin.

Here, where the summers are hotter and winters colder than on the coastal side, stately groves of ponderosa pine grow along with lodgepole pine and other hardy trees that harbor a wide variety of animal life. Although the trees of the eastside forests are not as dramatic in size as their westside counterparts, these ancient forests need protection, too. Some scientists believe that even more animal species are at risk here than in westside forests, because the eastside forests have already been so badly cut over.

the Pacific Northwest. To the east and west of Oregon's Willamette Valley, Douglas fir dominates the scene, stretching east from the coast as far as the crest of the Cascade Range, where it gives way to a drier, more extreme climate that favors ponderosa pine and other species. Continuing up the coastal range, the osprey traces its shadow over Douglas fir mixed with western red cedar and western hemlock. And in a narrow strip along the coast, it flies through fog over moisture-loving stands of Sitka spruce and hemlock. As the osprey crosses into British Columbia and wings north along the coast, it follows groves of spruce, hemlock and cedar from the water's edge all the way to the subalpine forest high in the steep coastal mountains. So it remains until the migrating bird reaches its breeding ground in the misty green forests of the Alaskan panhandle, where it fashions its nest in the broken top of an ancient spruce.

The lines between the varieties of forest aren't always clear. In some places, subtle changes of temperature and rainfall lead to a gradual thinning out of one species in favor of another, perhaps over a distance of a few hundred miles. Elsewhere, two different kinds of trees may be separated only by the line of a ridge.

Despite their differences, all of these forests have a few things in common. Unlike almost any other forests of the temperate zone (between the polar and equatorial regions), the ancient forests are dominated by cone-bearing trees called "conifers" – a far older family of plants than the flowering broadleaf trees such as oaks or maples. The forests are shaped by the copious moisture that flows off the Pacific, and the trees within them live for hundreds of years.

The climate of North America's West Coast is unique. Rainfall is plentiful, but it is concentrated in the fall, winter and spring. The summer is dry by comparison, putting deciduous trees – such as elms and beeches – at a disadvantage. So evergreen conifers dominate the scene. They benefit from a

THE TALE OF THE FALLEN TREE

Trees play an important role in the life cycle of the forest for centuries even after they die.

A tree that remains standing after it dies is called a "snag." Eagles and hawks perch on it while hunting. Owls, bats and woodpeckers use it to nest, store food and pass the winter. A large snag may stand, bleaching in the sun, for as long as a century.

When a dead tree falls to the ground, it adds diversity to the forest floor. Soil accumulates around it and small animals find shelter underneath. A porous decaying log can store critical moisture through the long, dry summers. Insects and fungi feed on it, and some fungi pump water from it to the roots of nearby trees. Eventually, the fallen tree becomes a "nurse log" to young seedlings that feed on its nutrients. A log can take as long to decompose as it took the tree to grow.

If the tree falls into a stream, it forms pools where young salmon and trout can hide from would-be predators. The insects that feed on these logs serve as food for the fish. The wood also slows the stream, minimizing erosion and trapping silt which would muddy the water. Even though logs in water decompose somewhat faster than on land, a log that fell into a stream when George Washington was president might still be there today.

So, when a tree falls in the forest and stays there, it still matters – to a bear that devours the termites eating its wood, to the trout that swims nearby or to the osprey that eats the trout for breakfast.

SALAMANDERS LARGE AND SMALL

It's hard to imagine a sala-mander eating anything as large as a frog or a mouse. But the Pacific giant salamander, a resident of the ancient forests, does just that. At near-ly a foot in length, it is the largest salamander on land and the major predator in many small streams. Its much smaller cousin, the Olympic salamander, lives on land but likes it wet. This rarest of California's amphibians finds shelter in moist, shady spots under rocks and fallen logs. Without the natural debris of the forest floor during the long, hot summers, these soft-bodied creatures would dry out and die.

temperate climate relatively free of the extremes of summer heat and hard winter freezes. Such conditions – and such forests – exist nowhere else on this conti-nent, and only in a few other spots in the world.

Not just old trees

The different species in the ancient forest depend on one another, making the whole greater than the sum of its parts. Ancient forests provide the best habitat for nearly 120 species of mammals, birds, amphibians and reptiles. More than 30 of these rely upon the ancient forests for nesting, breeding or feeding, and would suffer serious population losses without them. Some species might even go extinct.

As its name implies, a grove of trees takes a long time to become an "ancient forest." But it takes more than just old, living trees to make a forest ancient. The complete ecosystem that makes up our ancient forests consists of four other compo-nents, as well, which take more than a century to develop. When all five factors are present, the grove is classified as "old growth," the technical term for an ancient forest. These five factors are:

• At least two tree species with a range of ages and sizes, including several large, living Douglas firs or other coniferous trees that are at least 200 years old or greater than 32 inches in diameter;

• a forest canopy of many layers;

• several large, standing dead trees (called "snags");

• large logs on the forest floor; and

• large logs in streams.

Each of these elements of the forest contributes something vital. Three of them relate to trees that have already died. Snags provide hollow places for animals to nest and perch. Decaying logs on the forest floor enrich the soil, while offering food and shelter to hundreds of mammals and insects. And logs in streams provide pools and hiding places for fish. Thus the forest continues to be fed by the trees that have grown there in the past. A tree that toppled when Columbus sailed to America would only now be disappearing into the forest floor, leaving the younger trees to be

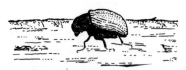

AN ENTERPRISING BEETLE

One clever forest insect, the ambrosia beetle, carries around the makings of its own supper inside its body. This fungus-eating, tunneling beetle transports the spores of a fungus that grows on the dead wood of fallen logs. When the insect settles in, the fungus does, too, providing a continuing source of food for the beetle.

SOIL IN THE SKY

So many fallen needles and animal droppings build up in the ancient forest's canopy that these branches become covered with a layer of organic "soil" more than an inch thick. This soil supports colonies of moss and lichen dozens of feet above the ground. Many animals, including the flying squirrel and the rufous hummingbird, use these beds of moss and lichen for their nests. One sea bird, the marbled murrelet, even flies ashore to nest in the tops of coastal ancient forests. It takes 150 years for enough moss and lichen to grow on a tree's branches to suit this bird, which depends upon the forest canopy for its survival.

nourished by its decaying wood.

These five aspects give the ancient forests their character. Younger forests may have one or two of these traits, but only the remarkably diverse ancient forests have them all.

Round and round

The life of the forest is woven of cycles. In the spring, as the sap starts to run and the trees emerge from their winter sleep, trees produce their light-colored "springwood." Then, as spring blends into summer and the soil becomes drier, they produce darker "summerwood." Successive bands of springwood and summerwood make the familiar pattern of rings on a tree that tells the story of the tree's lifetime. On the stump of a fallen tree, we can read the history of droughts and wildfires. We can trace the years of the tree's adolescence when it added an inch to its girth every year, and see how its growth slowed as it aged.

The food web – the who-eats-whom of nature – connects all living things in the forest. Squirrels and other rodents eat truffles containing the spores of certain fungi and spread them through the forest. These fungi ally themselves with tree roots and are essential to the trees' survival. One specialized rodent, the red tree vole, eats only the needles of the Douglas fir – and the spotted owl eats the vole. The deer browses on the young trees and brush, and the mosquito sips the deer's blood. The salmon hatchling snaps up the mosquito larva. Years later, returning from the sea, the salmon spawns and dies. Its body becomes food for raccoons and eagles, whose droppings fertilize the forest. The trees create the shade that keeps the water clear and cold enough for the salmon. These cycles make up the life of the forest.

Expecting the unexpected

The life of the forest changes in two ways: slowly and abruptly. Sudden events – such as a flood, fire or landslide – can reshape the ecosystem dramatically. The forest also changes very gradually, so that over several human lifetimes entirely different kinds of trees may take over the forest. How can the forest be ever-changing and be ancient at the same time? To understand this

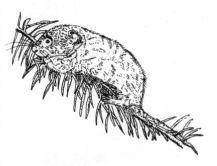

RED TREE VOLE

A red tree vole can live out its entire life without ever leaving the boughs of a single Douglas-fir tree. This highly specialized rodent eats the tree's leaves, lines its branch-top nest with uneaten scraps of fir needles, and drinks by licking rain and dew off the tree's foliage. Some researchers believe that red tree voles may reproduce for generations without ever leaving their ancestral family tree.

NOTES FROM UNDERGROUND

A few feet beneath the forest floor, the roots of a towering Douglas fir spread out, searching for water and nourishment. But the nutrients in the soil are so scattered that the roots can't do the job by themselves.

Fortunately, in one of the wondrous connections between the different parts of the forest, a family of fungi comes to the rescue. A "mycorrhizal fungus" is a special kind of organism that attaches itself to a root and sends out threads that scavenge water and minerals from the soil and provides this nourishment to the tree. In return, the tree – which makes sugar from sunlight – feeds the fungus. But that's not all. The fungus also covers the root and protects it from harmful infection, prolonging its life. Almost all plants form these symbiotic relationships, often with fungi that associate with that plant and no others. Trees cannot live without them. The fungi can even pass chemicals from one plant to another, leading some researchers to speculate that the webs of fungal filaments allow trees to feed off each other. Some scientists theorize that these filaments could serve as pathways for "communication" within the forest, signaling the presence of certain infestations by chemical code.

better, we need a concept from ecology called "succession."

On a freshly exposed patch of earth only enterprising plants can take hold. These are the kinds of plants that survive despite the harsh extremes of hot and cold, dry and wet that occur on bare soil. Often they are plants, such as grasses, that produce lots of seeds each year on the chance that such a site will become available. And their seeds must be able to travel from wherever their nearest colonies are.

These "pioneering" plants change the environment. They protect the ground from the harsh sun. Their roots break down rock into soil, and the leaves and stems that they shed each year create a fertile mulch. These changes allow new species of plants to thrive in the area. As time passes, seeds of more plant varieties arrive by chance. Often the newcomer plants will grow taller than the pioneering species and deprive them of the light they need to grow. So a whole new flora takes over – succeeding the pioneers. A site can undergo this process several times, with new plants dominating the scene each time. Different kinds of animals live in the habitat provided at each stage, so the animal population changes with succession as well.

Some stages in succession last a few months; others persist for centuries. At times, the shift from one stage to another takes place in a matter of seasons. In other cases, the changes occur so slowly that only very attentive researchers notice them. But unpredictable events such as tree-toppling windstorms and valley-scouring floods disrupt what might otherwise be a stately process. And more than any other natural disturbance, fire shapes the character of the Pacific forests.

Fire when ready

Every summer, the rain that falls steadily on the Northwest tapers off. Except for the far north and a narrow strip along the coast, the forest gets drier and becomes primed to burn. In a typical scenario in the Douglas-fir forest, thunderheads build up and a bolt of lightning strikes a tree or a snag, touching off the tinder of dead needles and twigs at its base.

Early in the season, the forest floor is still damp from winter rains. The fire licks gently along the ground, cleaning out the underbrush. It consumes the drier top layer of fallen needles and twigs (called "duff"), kills some seedlings and some of the less fire-resistant trees and shrubs. The fire might smolder for a few days, with flames rising no more than a foot high. Other than some charring of the forest floor, the forest is barely disturbed by a gentle fire such as this. In fact, it emerges even healthier. The nutrients of the charred plant life return to the soil to fertilize new growth. A mild burn reduces the amount of fuel in the forest and protects it, at least temporarily, from a much larger fire.

On a hotter day in late summer, however, when the underbrush on the forest floor is dry, a stray spark may ignite a major conflagration. If a fire hasn't been through this part of the forest in a century or more, there is plenty of fuel available – from the forest floor to dry moss on the tree trunks to the canopy hundreds of feet above. A small fire jumps from the duff into the dry branches on the ground. Fanned by a hot wind, the blaze easily kindles the dry snags in its path, causing them to explode into fire and shower sparks and flaming wood

FIRE HAS ITS PLACE

A fire is nature's way of giving some trees and shrubs their turn. California's redwood, for example, has thick fibrous bark that insulates it from heat. The trees that grow nearby are not as well protected, so fire has helped to create the now-famous stands of redwoods. Many other plants – such as blueblossom, snowbrush and manzanita – can't reproduce at all without fire. The seeds of these shrubs wait in the soil by the millions until a fire cracks their shells. Similarly, the cones of certain pines are sealed shut with a sticky resin that melts and releases their seeds only in a hot fire.

Without an occasional intense fire, Douglas firs might have been taken over by cedars and hemlocks long ago. The seedlings of these competing trees survive better in the shade. So when a raging fire sweeps through the forest and kills most of the trees, it allows sunlight to reach the forest floor, giving the Douglas fir a chance to become re-established.

Unfortunately, by putting out fires as often as possible during the last century, we've let the underbrush accumulate to a dangerous degree, setting the stage for conflagrations that will blacken larger areas, making natural recovery more difficult. Forest Service ecologist Tom Atzet compares this practice to holding your finger over the end of a hose: "You don't know how long you can keep it there, but you know that eventually the water will squirt out."

in all directions. These firebrands set new fires, roaring up 250-foot trees, leaping into the canopy and marching on, setting everything in their path aflame. A burn such as this will continue until the weather changes.

Such a fire completely transforms the forest. Some trees are blackened from ground to top and some have fallen. Others have burned to the ground, marked by a ghostly pile of white ash and a pit where the fire burned down to the roots. A few trees survive unscathed. Others seem only slightly scorched, but the fire has killed the layer of living cells beneath their bark, so these trees are bound to die. But as devastating as such a fire may seem, this is not the end of the forest's story.

Starting over

As summer turns to fall, the cones of the dying trees and the remaining live ones finish ripening. Cones burst open, scattering winged seeds across the charred forest. Rodents find some of them. Other seeds survive and some take root. The first spring after the fire brings an outburst of new life. Snowbrush seeds pop open, awakened by the fire after lying in the soil for decades. Grasses and other plants that were unable to grow in the deep shade of the old forest once again sprout amid the blackened snags. Green plants begin to dot the landscape, providing forage for deer and elk, as well as smaller animals and their predators. Within a decade or so, other shrubs begin to take over. Snowbrush and alder help turn nitrogen from the air into plant nutrients, fertilizing the soil.

Meanwhile, Douglas-fir seedlings sprout in the partial sun, shaded by snags. But they need more than sun to survive. They need soil, and they need "mycorrhizal fungi," a special type of fungus that attaches itself to roots, helping trees absorb the soil's nutrients. Fortunately, some of these fungi can live on the roots of the madrone, snowbrush and other shrubs that survive the fire while the new Douglas firs are becoming established. In addition, the fungi's spores can be carried in the droppings of rodents. If a Douglas-fir seedling is lucky, its roots will encounter a spore-bearing pellet, which will help the young tree obtain the nourishment it needs. If the seedling is unlucky and fails to meet any fungi, it will die.

As the trees continue to grow, more creatures return to the recovering forest. The red tree vole may adopt a Douglas fir in which to live once the tree is 25 or 30 years old. The western red-backed vole and the flying squirrel, two other distinctive inhabitants of the coastal forests, will spend more time in the new forest once the fungi are more plentiful.

As the trees grow taller, the canopy begins to grow thick, keeping the earth below quite dark. From about age 30 to age 100, the forest looks like a very uniform place, with Douglas-fir trees of about the same age and size, punctuated by taller trees that survived the fire. As the community ages, it becomes more diverse. By the time it reaches the middle of its second century, the dense canopy of conical Douglas firs has been replaced by a grove of larger and less uniformly spaced trees supporting a wide variety of plant and animal life. After two centuries, this once-burned forest is mature and complex enough to be called ancient again.

A forest landscape is patchy. At any moment in time, some patches may be young, many areas are ancient, and some are in-between. These patches may be large or small, clustered or far apart, depending on the natural events that formed them – wildfires, lightning strikes, high winds that knock down trees, or the natural falling of old snags that creates openings in the forest. Just as an individual tree sprouts, grows, ages and dies, so, too, a forest passes through stages of succession. Forests at all of these stages are called "native" or "natural" if they arose without logging or planting. For the area to be healthy, there must be groves in each stage. If only ancient forest existed, where would the seeds of grasses and shrubs come from to colonize land that had recently burned? If young forest were all there was, where would the animals live that need old forests? In the same way that communities of people thrive when there is a mixture of children, young adults and older people, so a landscape of forests needs to include all ages.

More to learn

Our understanding of the connections described here is primarily the result of only about 25 to 30 years of research, and more knowledge is being gained each year. In another quarter century, we may look back and be amazed at how little of the forest we now understand. But we do know that the connections between the parts are at least this complex and of humbling intricacy. Although many of the details have changed, the old-growth forests that we see now have grown, burned and regrown for a very long time. Forest Service ecologist Tom Atzet is fond of asking foresters how long they think the Douglas fir has existed. "Some of them say, 'Since the ice ages,'" Atzet says. "But the fact is, Douglas fir has been recognizable from its pollen for the last 15 million years. Conifer relatives of the Douglas fir were well established in the Triassic period, 200 million years ago."

The ancient forests are still grand and awe-inspiring – even though a major percentage of them has been logged. Human beings have cut down all but a fraction of the ancient forests in the last 100 years alone. The next chapter explores the reasons to care about and protect our remaining ancient forest legacy.

DIVERSITY
OF LIFE

DIVERSITY OF LIFE

Why care about ancient forests?

We are part of the forest. For much of our species' life span, forest covered the land. In our deepest imaginations, our myths and our dreams, we are inextricably bound up in it. To reawaken this knowledge is to become aware of how important it is to preserve our remaining ancient forests.

The native peoples who first lived on this continent understood that they inhabited the land in relationship to everything else that grew and lived here, and that their very existence rested upon that interdependency. Westward-bound pioneers had a different attitude. With their "can do" American spirit, they saw the wild lands as something to be mastered, and they treated virgin forests as if they existed solely to meet human demands. To them, the forests were inexhaustible and there for the cutting – and cut them they did.

Today, with the limits of the ancient forests clearly in sight, the philosophy of balance is re-emerging – the notion that our environment is a web of life, and that we humans are members of the forest community. This modern-day "land ethic," described in 1949 by conservationist Aldo Leopold, suggests that natural systems should be treated with love and respect. By so doing, we ensure the survival not just of the earth (which got along just fine before we showed up), but of humanity, as well.

Our planet teems with an astonishing array of plant and animal life. Preserving this "biological diversity" (or "biodiversity") is essential to protecting the ancient forests. When we endanger the lives of forest creatures, such as marbled murrelets, tailed frogs – even fungi – we endanger the community of life and, ultimately, our own future as a species.

Recreation, inspiration and scientific discovery

Protecting ancient forests is a very practical goal, since the ancient forests are fundamental to the vitality of the region. People place a high value on such values as clean air and water and accessible areas of superb natural beauty. Indeed, these characteristics encourage businesses to locate in the Pacific Northwest and can help to sustain the region's economy as logging ceases to be its mainstay. These desirable qualities also lure visitors. In 1988, recreation contributed $6 billion to the economies of Washington and Oregon alone.

But the forests provide more than a wonderful place for people to live, work, play or seek inspiration. They also sustain a wealth of biodiversity. A single tree in the ancient forest may shelter as many as 1,500 invertebrates. Any ancient forests species may hold the clue to an important scientific discovery. Since researchers have been intensively studying these forests only since the late 1960s, no one knows how many untold secrets the forests might contain.

Learning forestry from the forests

Another kind of scientific knowledge we can gain from the ancient forests is how to manage all forests more intelligently.

THE VERY USEFUL YEW

Pacific yew trees grow very slowly in the shade of the ancient forest.

Restricted to cool, moist habitats, the yew is one of the slowest growing trees in the world, taking as long as 50 years to increase in diameter by one inch.

The small size of the yew belies its importance. Its bark contains a powerful cancer-fighting chemical called taxol. The drug stops cancer cells from multiplying and has shown promising results in clinical trials that began in 1984. These studies indicate that taxol may be extremely effective in treating advanced ovarian cancer and may also be important in treating breast cancer, lung cancer and other forms of the disease.

Because the yew's existence is ultimately linked to ancient forests, and such a large proportion of these forests have already been destroyed by logging operations, the valuable yew is already at risk. But neither the U.S. Forest Service nor the Bureau of Land Management has made any provisions to protect it. In fact, in January 1991, the U. S. Fish and Wildlife Service denied a petition by a coalition of environmental groups to list the Pacific yew as a threatened species.

At a conference on taxol sponsored by the National Cancer Institute in June 1990, researchers reported that "clinical development of taxol has been limited by the shortage of drug available to conduct clinical trials" and "further development will depend on solving problems of supply." Protecting that supply – as well as the existence of other medical benefits that may await discovery in the future – means protecting the ancient forest on which the yew relies.

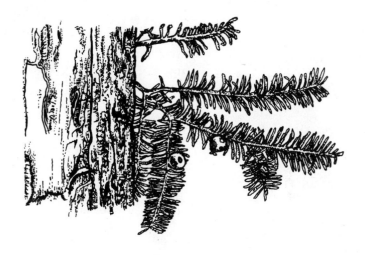

Foresters have devised techniques to produce the greatest amount of timber in the shortest possible time, but none of these methods has been tested over the long haul. The place with the longest recorded experience at managing forests is Central Europe, where the Germans have been practicing scientific forestry since the early 19th century. But in recent years a mysterious malady, called *Waldsterben* (forest death), has developed in those forests, caused by bad forest practices combined with air pollution. After two crops of timber have been harvested from the site, successive plantings don't grow as well. The same is true in Australia, in forests of Monterey pine. The forests of the Pacific Northwest have been logged for an even shorter time, so we still don't know what the long-range effects of our current forestry practices might be.

Ancient forests are a proven way of growing trees. For thousands of years, virgin forests have grown in the places where they now stand. As we begin to understand them, we can learn what we need to know about raising timber over the long term. We can also gain a better understanding of the ecological community of which we are a part.

FOG DRIP

Believe it or not, trees can actually pull water out of clouds. Forest Service researchers in Oregon found that 35 percent of the annual precipitation in the region they studied came from fog that condensed onto the needles of the tall trees and dripped down to the forest floor. In Northern California, the redwood forests wring 7 to 12 inches of "fog drip" out of the sky each year, mostly during the rainless summer when the trees need it most.

Undoubtedly, many more discoveries about the ancient forests await the attention of tomorrow's researchers – which is why it is so important not to destroy the original "working models."

Clean water, clean air

Even more important than the pleasure we may derive from walking through a magnificent old forest, or the scientific knowledge we may gain there, is the long-term value the forest provides in regulating the earth's climate and protecting our watersheds.

When rain falls on the forest, it percolates down through leaves and branches to the forest floor. If the rain falls instead on a large area that has been stripped of trees – a technique called "clearcutting" – the bare ground of the clearcut receives the full force of the rain, and soil washes into the streams. Mud and silt can sully the water, endangering fish and increasing the risk of flooding. In the Pacific Northwest, where intense rainstorms can drop several inches of water a day, run-off can easily scour soil from the hillsides and cause rivers to overflow their banks.

Ancient forests hold moisture, remaining cool and damp long after a rain. Clearcuts can reduce the humidity in the air, affecting the climate of the surrounding forest and robbing young trees of much-needed moisture. In California, scientists found that 1 1/2 times as much water evaporates from exposed soil as from the shaded ground of a mature forest.

Ancient forests protect the land and the rivers. The forest's canopy and the thick layers of duff shield the ground from the force of the raindrops. Roots hold the soil in place on steep slopes. After roots decay, they leave behind channels that allow run-off to soak into the soil instead of coursing across the earth and washing it away. Burrowing animals, such as squirrels, leave behind similar drainage tunnels. Also, the stout branches of ancient trees can support large quantities of snow, which allows it to melt slowly instead of piling up on the ground. That way, if a warm rain follows a snowstorm, catastrophic flooding is less likely because the snow will have already melted.

TAILED FROG

Tailed frogs put in a three-year apprenticeship as tadpoles before they become adults – unlike most frogs, which mature in a single season. They thrive only in the shaded, cool water of the ancient forests. Most logging washes silt into the creeks where the frogs live and exposes the water to the sun, making it too warm for them to survive.

THE FISH AND THE FOREST

Salmon have migrated between the creeks and the sea for thousands of years.

Their eggs, which are laid in the gravel of streambeds, are nearly pea-sized and bright orange. The eggs hatch in three or four months and the salmon fry swim into the stream where they stay for six months to two years, feeding on insects and crustaceans.

Instinct then draws them to the sea. Migrating in schools through the North Pacific, they swim from as far south as California all the way to the Bering Sea, fattening themselves on shrimp, squid and other sea animals.

After one to four years, the urge to spawn compels them home. Guided by the scent of the waters where they hatched, they navigate to the mouth of the same river and creek where they began. By now they are sleek, firm and "at the peak of their physical and instinctual genius," as Freeman House wrote in his classic essay, "Totem Salmon."

Once they re-enter fresh water, the salmon live only on their stores of body fat. At up to 50 pounds each, they leap upstream over rapids and small waterfalls. In Alaska, where salmon runs are near their primordial levels, creeks may be choked with their bright flashing bodies. Some fish fall prey to predators, but enough survive the journey to pair up en route for the mating that follows.

When they reach the spawning grounds, the female flaps her tail to scoop out a nest in the streambed and deposits her eggs as the male fertilizes them. She then covers the eggs with gravel. Having achieved their purpose, the adult salmon soon die, leaving behind the eggs of the fittest among them.

Swimming upstream

The clean water that flows out of the ancient forests is crucial for fish. The Native Americans who originally lived in this area depended on salmon as a major food source. Today, salmon fishing is a multibillion-dollar industry for the region, from Alaska to Northern California. The survival of these fish is intricately linked to healthy forests. And, although salmon can be propagated in hatcheries, their natural spawning is a vital part of evolution and the ecological chain. Many animals – raccoon, osprey, bear and eagle, among others – eat the spawning salmon.

Salmon survive best in cold water, between 40 and 60 degrees Fahrenheit. Cutting the trees around a stream allows sunlight to reach the water, warming it considerably beyond this range. The water can easily get so warm – in the mid- to high 70s – that it kills the fish.

What's more, salmon need clean water. If silt washes into the creek, filling up the spaces in the gravel beds where salmon make their nests, it can suffocate the salmon eggs and clog the gills of those hatchlings that do emerge. Ancient forests minimize these risks by reducing erosion, as well as providing fallen logs which create pools for fish and harbor insects that the fish eat.

PACIFIC DAMPWOOD TERMITE

We rely on green plants to turn carbon dioxide into oxygen. And plants rely on soil bacteria to turn nitrogen in the air into nitrate fertilizer. The Pacific dampwood termite, which helps decompose dead wood in the forest, couldn't survive without the help of two kinds of bacteria that inhabit its gut. One type ferments the wood that the termite eats, producing acetic acid (vinegar) that the termite can digest. The other extracts nitrogen from the air and converts it to a form that nourishes the first bacteria as well as the termite.

Salmon can also spawn in streams that run through younger forests. But the rate at which the forests are being cut and the logging methods that have been used – along with dams that block the salmon's spawning migrations, erosion from ranching, past over-fishing and urban pollution – have drastically reduced salmon populations overall.

Keeping us out of the greenhouse

Human beings cannot put a price on the vital work that plant life performs in maintaining a liveable climate for all of the earth's creatures. A growing forest removes carbon dioxide from the air in a process common to all green plants, called "photosynthesis." Plants use the energy in sunlight to pull carbon dioxide from the air and use it to build their roots, trunks, branches and leaves. In the process, they release oxygen into the atmosphere. A single acre of temperate forest is an incredible oxygen factory, giving off more than 6 tons of oxygen every year.

In an ancient forest, decomposition is an ongoing process. Snags, downed logs and dead needles decay; and the organisms that eat them take in oxygen and breathe out carbon dioxide. This cycle was once in balance, with as much carbon dioxide being consumed by plants as was exhaled by animals and bacteria. But the cycle has been seriously out of balance since the 19th century. The burning of fossil fuels dumps more carbon dioxide into the air than the plants can remove. In addition, people have leveled the forests and burned the logs or let them decay. As a result, most of the carbon that was stored in the wood was released into the air as carbon dioxide. Deforestation, together with the burning of fossil fuels, has raised the amount of carbon dioxide in the air by more than 25 percent since the mid-19th century. In a process known as the "greenhouse effect," this colorless, odorless gas traps heat near the earth's surface, preventing the heat from escaping into space. The more carbon dioxide, the warmer the climate. After a series of rigorous studies, most scientists now believe that the world is risking devastating changes in the earth's climate as a result of higher carbon dioxide levels.

The ancient forests store carbon, preventing it from escaping to

CUTTING DOWN ON GOOD AIR

When one acre of ancient forest is logged, about as much carbon dioxide is released as 200 cars driven for one year. The 60,000 acres of ancient forests logged in Oregon and Washington each year account for more carbon dioxide than is produced by all the cars in Southern California.

FOREST-LOVING FLOWERS

Plants in the heath and orchid families called "saprophytes" don't make their own food from sunlight, as most plants do. They subsist on the decay of plant matter in the soil. The decaying logs they feed on are found mainly in ancient forests.

the air as carbon dioxide. Acre for acre, ancient forests contain more carbon than any other land-based ecosystem. But when an area is logged, three-quarters of the carbon stored in trees, leaves and fallen logs is released into the atmosphere, contributing to the greenhouse effect.

A glimpse of nature's secrets

The ancient forest holds many mysteries about adaptation and survival that we are just beginning to understand. Some animals, such as the marbled murrelet and western red-backed vole along with its cousin, the red tree vole, have needs met only by centuries-old forests. Woodpeckers, owls, raccoons and bats need a forest old enough to have snags, where they make their homes. Sitka black-tailed deer use the ancient forests as shelter from the winter's bitter cold and deep snow. Specialized plants, such as the yew tree and certain plants in the orchid family, also thrive especially well in the environment of the ancient forests.

Other organisms' reliance on ancient forests appears to be much more subtle. Roosevelt elk, for example, are mainly found outside the ancient forests, but they take shelter there during harsh winters – or to evade predators. Timber managers have touted logging as a boon for deer and elk because it opens up the land to grasses on which the animals browse. While this may have been an advantage a century ago when more of the ancient forest remained, now there's no shortage of habitat for deer and elk, but there is a significant lack of habitat for animals that depend on the ancient forest. Tree plantations don't improve the situation, even from the elks' point of view. When the plantation is very young, heavy snows may build up on the ground so thickly that the elk cannot feed. As the trees grow, they crowd out the plants on which elk browse.

Scientists are still trying to understand precisely how animals rely on the ancient forests. Some creatures spend their whole lives there. Others feed elsewhere but reproduce only in the ancient forest. Populations of some animals in younger groves may depend on immigration from the ancient forests, and might wither away without the "parent" forests to supply new immigrants.

READING ABOUT RIGHTS

Following philosophical and legal lines of reasoning, some authors have attributed rights to the forest similar to those of human beings. If that idea intrigues you, you might consider reading:

• **The Arrogance of Humanism**
by David Ehrenfeld (Oxford University Press, 1978). This book makes the case that most people are too quick to believe that technology can solve whatever problems may appear in nature.

• **Deep Ecology**
edited by George Sessions and Bill Devall (Peregrine Smith Books, 1985). This book explores the intrinsic value of natural ecological communities and how they are seen by varous wings of the environmental movement.

• **Should Trees Have Standing?**
by Christopher D. Stone (W. Kaufmann Inc., 1974). The author considers the implications of granting to natural objects and beings the right to be represented in court.

RESTING ON OUR TOPSOIL

A society's survival rests on the quality of its topsoil

– or so say Vernon Gill Carter and Tom Dale in their classic book, *Topsoil and Civilization*. Topsoil provides the food, fiber and timber that allows the rest of the culture to exist. What's more, they argue, past civilizations persisted only as long as their soil was fertile.

Ancient civilizations began when people were well supplied with their basic needs and could devote attention to other pursuits, such as art, writing and astronomy. Fertile soil permitted a few people to reap a harvest big enough for all.

Through history, Carter and Dale found case after case in which a nation used up the fertility of its soil and fell from power. The Greeks, the Romans and the North Africans suffered this fate. The mighty cedars of Lebanon, used by the Phoenicians for building ships and temples, were reduced by the mid-1970s to four small groves. The authors show that even when nations were vanquished by foreign tribes, they were able to recover quickly if the soil was healthy. If it had been stripped and eroded, however, the civilizations often began to deteriorate as well.

Soil building is a slow process. It can take a thousand years to form an inch of soil. That inch can erode in a decade if the earth is exposed and the roots of the cut trees decay before new roots grow to hold the soil in place. If we don't stop treating our soil like dirt, history tells us we'll end up on the ash heap of civilization.

We do know that natural disturbances – such as landslides, fires, droughts and floods – are part of the forest's life, and that these events often abruptly reduce the amount of habitat for ancient forest species. More than a bare minimum of habitat must be preserved so that the forest's animals can survive such disturbances. To protect less than this is to risk the extinction of these species after the inevitable fire or windstorm.

A diverse forest is an evolving forest

Just because all these animals depend on the ancient forests, why should we go out of our way to protect them? For one thing, each individual plant and animal is unique. Every one carries tens of thousands of pieces of genetic information that have evolved for millions of years to adapt to present environmental conditions. By protecting the forest, we're protecting a vast storehouse of genetic material and safeguarding a process that has been going on since the first spark of life in the primordial soup 3 billion years ago.

Ancient forests maintain and regulate themselves through an ecological diversity which provides countless built-in controls. If a natural disturbance threatens the status quo, internal regulators often act to correct it. For example, if a population explosion of red tree voles occurs, the owls that prey on them may fledge more young who will eat the voles, thus reducing the rodents' numbers to a manageable level. Different species provide these checks and balances in different ways, and they are all necessary for the ancient forests to function smoothly.

The genetic variation between species gives the forest greater staying power to withstand minor disturbances, such as an especially cold winter or pest infestation. Even major events – such as fire, windstorms and floods – are only temporary setbacks, at worst. Some individuals will be able to tolerate the new circumstances better than others. Those who survive will pass on these hardy features to their offspring. In such innumerable ways as these, the forest continues to renew itself.

Left alone, the forests have proven that they can adapt and survive almost anything, except human abuse. If we want the ancient forests to continue to thrive, we must turn from being their destroyers to being their students. We can learn many things from the forests, not the least of which is a more realistic sense of our place within the ecosystem. All of the myriad features and functions of the forest affect us as a species. In the next chapter, we will see how the attitudes and actions of people threaten the continued existence of our ancient forests.

THREE

THREATS TO THE ANCIENT FOREST

THREATS TO THE ANCIENT FOREST

The destruction of a precious resource

With four generations of timber-workers in his family, logging the woods is in George Atiyeh's blood. He co-founded a timber company in the 1970s and within a few years was running a sawmill in the fertile forest country of the Oregon Cascades. "We thought we could cut forever and not make a dent in it," he recalls from an armchair at home in a mill town east of Salem, Oregon. But when he flew a small plane over the land he'd been logging, Atiyeh changed his mind. From the air he could see that the entire forest was being leveled. "I didn't want to be responsible for the destruction of the last old-growth forests," he says. Atiyeh sold his business and began working to preserve a grove that was special to him, along Opal Creek in the Willamette National Forest. Eight years later, despite Forest Service efforts to cut it, the grove remains unlogged, thanks to the vigilance of Atiyeh and others, and is among the largest unprotected stands of ancient forest in the Cascades.

The ancient forests are imperiled throughout their range, from southeastern Alaska to California's Sierra Nevada. Timber companies, with the blessing of federal and provincial agencies, log and replace them with tree farms lacking the diversity and life cycle of a natural forest. What little remains is split into ever-smaller groves by logging and road-building, fragmenting the habitat of creatures that need large expanses of old-growth forest to survive. As the fragmentation process continues, small patches of ancient forest become virtually useless to the plants and animals that need them. If present practices continue unchecked, the fragmented remnants of the ancient forests will be worthless as habitat within two decades. In this chapter, we'll explore the threat to the forest and some of the pressures that fuel it.

Race to the saw

When American pioneers first came to the west coast of North America, they found vast tracts of primeval forest, covering some 45 million acres. For the first hundred years, crude technology, the massive trees and rough terrain limited loggers to the most accessible areas. But after World War II, the widespread use of the bulldozer and chainsaw made it possible to cut in more remote areas and to step up the pace of logging. Within a few decades, privately owned forests were virtually all logged and those on public land severely threatened.

In western Oregon and Washington, an estimated 19 million acres of natural forest once spread across the land. Barely 10 percent of the original ancient forest remains, primarily on federal lands – national parks, national forests and lands administered by the Bureau of Land Management. About a third of these groves have been so isolated by logging in surrounding areas that they can no longer support the full complement of life native to the ancient forests.

In California, just 8 percent of the ancient coastal redwoods still stand. Sixty percent of British Columbia's coastal old-

WHAT'S LEFT?

Recent studies by two environmental groups show that much less ancient forest remains than had been previously thought. A preliminary survey by The Wilderness Society found less than half as much old growth as the U.S. Forest Service had claimed on six national forests in western Oregon and Washington. By inspecting a random sample of the forest, researchers found that many areas with large trees didn't have other elements of old growth, such as snags and downed logs. The Society then prepared new maps using satellite photos and computerized mapping. The results were so precise that even the Forest Service had to accept their validity.

In the Seattle office of The Wilderness Society, a computer image shows an outline of a proposed spotted owl sanctuary. By pushing another button, a map of old-growth groves is superimposed over the drawing. One can instantly see which part of the ancient forest would be protected and which would not.

The National Audubon Society took a different tack. Under its Adopt-a-Forest program, it funded grassroots groups around the Northwest to map old-growth regions from the ground. Equipped with standard aerial photographs of the national forests, Audubon's trained volunteers recorded their observations with tools as basic as felt markers and sheets of clear acetate.

In her office in Ashland, Oregon, Julie Norman – executive director of the forest activist group, Headwaters – displays maps of the Rogue National Forest. As she opens the map boards, the story unfolds in a crazy-quilt pattern of reds (for logged areas) and greens (for uncut regions). Besides the importance of knowing where the ancient forests remain, says Norman, the process of map-making and getting to know the forest more intimately spurred many citizens to become more involved in the issue.

growth forest is gone, and the rest is being destroyed so fast that all but a small percentage will be gone by the year 2020 if the pace keeps up. Loggers in British Columbia often leave behind a quarter of the marketable timber in their haste to remove the most valuable trees.

Many irreplaceable, magnificent groves are still falling, and have yet to receive systematic protection. In Washington, Oregon and California, less than a third of them are off-limits to logging, and the parts that are not safeguarded are slated to be logged or further fragmented within the next decade or two. Overall, just a small percentage of the original forest has received protection. Most of this is at high elevations, in less productive areas that could be set aside at less cost to the timber industry. These higher-altitude forests also provide habitat for fewer species than low-elevation stands.

The entire ancient-forest ecosystem is in danger. Although some scientists argue that the ancient forests could grow back, given undisturbed

OUR DIMINISHING VIRGIN FORESTS

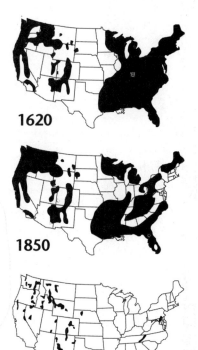

1620

1850

1990

centuries, human beings are not permitting them to do so. And without protection, species that are part of the old-growth ecology would become extinct.

Throughout the forests, the history of logging has followed a familiar pattern. First the timber companies logged their own land faster than it could grow back. Then they turned to federal forests to tide them over until their next stand of trees was ready. This is especially true for old-growth timber. Most private firms exhausted their ancient forests decades ago, and now depend on the government for a supply of large trees. During the 1980s, lumber companies kept up the pressure on federal agencies to provide them with the timber they demanded. Time and again, these pressures were passed on to Congress, which directed the agencies to sell more timber for logging than agency foresters believed the forest could sustain.

A clear-cut case

The forests are not only being logged too quickly, they're being completely transformed. Whole forests are clearcut, every tree removed, leaving a field of stumps

FORESTS? I SAY 'BULLY!'

The U.S. Forest Service was created in 1905 under the administration of conservation-minded President Theodore Roosevelt. He designated so much land as national forest – thereby excluding it from immediate logging – that the lumber barons pressed Congress to pass a law eliminating his power to do so. In the week before he signed that bill into law, Roosevelt protected an additional 16 million acres.

where the area once teemed with verdant life. Roads are punched across the hillsides for hauling logs. Bulldozers track up and down the steep slopes, gouging and compacting the land with their steel treads. Cables drag logs up the hills, disheveling the soil. And finally, loggers burn the "slash" – the branches, needles and tops of trees too small to mill or pulp. The result is a wrecked and charred landscape, about as welcoming to ancient-forest denizens as the encrusted bottom of an oven. Squirrels, salamanders and other animals that depend on tall trees, logs and mushrooms common to the ancient forests die because they have no homes and no food.

Clearcuts are without precedent in nature. One Forest Service scientist tells of a presentation he gave on forest ecology. "The next slide contains a list of all the natural processes replicated by clearcutting," he said, building up suspense. The slide was blank.

If just one small tract suffered this fate, the forest's creatures would simply move elsewhere. However, vast areas of the ancient forest have been logged in this way or are scheduled to be cut.

NATIVE INTELLIGENCE

The Native American peoples of the Pacific Northwest took material from the forest without damaging it. They used cedar bark to make rope, baskets and items of clothing, and carved cedar planks from tree trunks to build their longhouses. In each case, they left the tree standing. Only when they needed to carve a totem pole or build a dugout canoe did they fell an entire tree.

The result: drastic reductions in the population of plants and animals that depend on the ancient groves, more threatened species and less diversity within the forest.

Clearcuts affect the neighboring forest, too. Exposed soil washes down the hillside with the winter run-off into the streams below. Trees at the edge of the cut are vulnerable to being blown down by winter gales or scalded by the sun. Animals such as the spotted owl that need the shelter of the deep forest are exposed to their natural enemies that prowl the edge of the woods. Creatures that require a larger range and can't cross over the clearcut are trapped.

On the western side of the Cascades, on Washington's Olympic Peninsula, the forests are so mangily fragmented by clearcuts that they resemble moth-eaten sweaters. Some of the holes have grown even larger than the remaining fabric.

Tree farms don't fill the gap

Defenders of clearcutting and the timber industry's other forest practices like to claim that their approach is just fine because the trees will grow back. Timber companies run ads boasting about the millions of seedlings they have planted. But it isn't that simple. Tree plantations (or "tree farms," as they're often called) may produce a relatively quick yield of timber, but ecologically, they cannot take the place of a natural forest. Tree farms differ in crucial ways from the forests that came before them. They completely transform the landscape, making it inhospitable to most creatures of the forest.

Tree farms lack the key stages of a natural forest's early development and must run a gauntlet of hazards that can kill the trees before they mature. Frequently, the slash in a clearcut is burned and the nutrients stored there go up in smoke instead of decaying into the soil. Scientists have shown that this practice reduces the soil's fertility, decreasing its ability to grow trees. Then timber companies, the Bureau of Land Management and the Forest Service plant seedlings of their favorite commercial species (mostly Douglas fir).

If the seedlings manage to survive the baking summer heat of the exposed clearcut, the young plantation forest is still less diverse than a natural one. Favoring the planted trees, tree-farm managers beat back the brush and hardwoods that try to take root among them. But broadleaf plants are a natural part of the life cycle in many forests. To eliminate them is to deprive the forest of an essential phase in its development. Snowbrush and alder enrich the soil, and madrone and manzanita keep alive the fungi that the Douglas fir need. Without them, biological loops in the forest are broken, and the forest is less able to support a variety of life.

Growers often plant "improved" varieties of conifers that are fast growing. But because they lack the diversity of natural stands – sharing the same weaknesses as well as strengths – these trees may actually be more vulnerable to certain infesta-

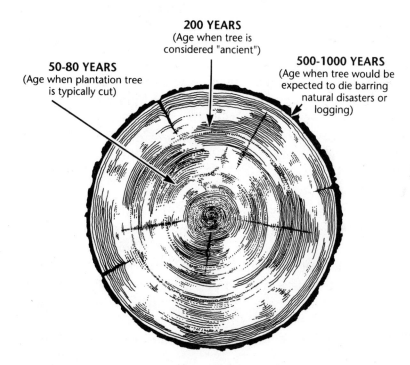

200 YEARS
(Age when tree is considered "ancient")

50-80 YEARS
(Age when plantation tree is typically cut)

500-1000 YEARS
(Age when tree would be expected to die barring natural disasters or logging)

tions and illnesses. Tree farms are also extremely vulnerable to fire. In a recent blaze in southern Oregon, 27 out of 29 plantations burned intensely, compared with a much lower fraction of the natural forests. If the plantation burns, it is usually replanted in the same uniform way.

Plantations are generally scheduled to be logged after 50 to 80 years, long before the 200 years that must pass before a forest begins to regain the characteristics of an ancient grove. They never attain the same age, dignity and complexity as the virgin forests they have replaced. Gone are the thick boughs, laden with moss and lichen, and the rich variety of plant and animal life beneath them. Gone are the deep cracks in the bark of fallen logs that offered shelter for insects and nourishment for spores and seedlings. The plantation is more like a cornfield than a forest.

Most of our ancient forests have already been logged and converted to tree plantations, and it's too late to save them – at least within our lifetimes. Timber may be a renewable resource, as a bumper sticker seen on pick-up trucks in the Northwest proclaims. But even if no more old-growth trees were cut, it would still take two centuries for today's tree farms to begin to resemble ancient forests and provide homes for species that depend on them.

As devastating as the harsh reality of this situation is, the ancient forests that exist today are not just the only ones left – they are the only ones that the next eight generations of humanity will ever know.

The timber industry justifies the creation of tree farms as a way to produce the wood that society demands. But many scientists doubt that they are a reliable way of doing that because, without natural ecological processes, the plantations themselves are not sustainable. "In the long term, I don't see that this model has proven it's going to work," warns ecologist Atzet. "If we follow it, we're making a grave mistake."

Even timber industry workers admit that the forests have

THE ROAD TO NOWHERE

Logging roads do more damage to the forest than anything except the actual act of clearcutting.

Roads fragment the ancient forest. Even if they just cross a grove en route to a distant logging site, the grove becomes less useful to the creatures of the old-growth forest. Roads also speed up erosion in several ways, ultimately washing soil off hillsides and into creeks and rivers. Roads disrupt the flow of water down the hillside, concentrating it in ways that carve gullies in the ground and trigger landslides. If roads aren't maintained during the wet season – and few are – the culverts that conduct water under the road may clog with leaves and other debris. Water will run over the top of the road and wash it out, sending more silt into the streams below. Finally, the fill used to build a road can slide right off the hill, especially when it's saturated with rain.

This erosion causes harm in two ways: It washes away fertile topsoil and it pollutes the streams it drains into. At 365,000 miles, the Forest Service road system is eight times longer than the U.S. interstate highway network. But the agency is still at it. In 1989, it committed about $175 million to road construction.

The solution is to build fewer roads, leave roadless areas alone, close roads where they are no longer needed and maintain them properly if they're still in use.

been mismanaged. Says Oregon millworker Mike Morgan, "Sure, we made mistakes. A man who doesn't fall on his face isn't moving forward. But if I thought we'd continue to 'rape and destroy,' I'd be on the other side of the fence in a New York second. After all, who would want to see the forest flourish more than we would? Our livelihoods depend on it."

They want it all now

No matter how good the workers' intentions, they don't control forest policy – the timber industry does, and timber firms are driven by the bottom line. Short-term profit is their priority, not forests. And in today's marketplace, that means turning trees into dollars as quickly as possible. Mature trees tend to grow at a slower rate than money in the bank, so most investors will cut the tree and put the money to work making more money. Two firms that used to buck this trend – Oregon's Medco and California's Pacific Lumber – became targets of hostile takeovers during the 1980s. That scared other publicly held companies, and few since have dared to deviate from the standard of quick cutting for quick profits.

The rationale of short-term gain leads private companies to liquidate their old growth as quickly as they can sell it. For the same reason, they clearcut when they log. As Harry Merlo, chief executive of Louisiana-Pacific, told an interviewer, "There shouldn't be anything left on the ground [after logging].... We log to infinity. Because we need it all. It's ours. It's out there, and we need it all. Now."

It's easy to understand why these companies see cash when they look at an ancient forest. Individual trees can be worth several thousand dollars each. The timber on an acre of ancient forest is valued at $40,000 to $80,000. Redwood fetches more than $100,000 per acre. The yield from a single acre could build as many as 20 three-bedroom houses. What's more, it's all nature's bounty. No one paid to prepare the site, plant the trees, or take care of them. All human beings have to do is cut them down and haul them away.

This desire for high, short-term returns is in direct conflict with the natural forest, which grows slowly over the long term. Modern-day timber firms have tried to mold the forest to suit the quick profits they seek, rather than changing the expectations of their venture to suit the pace of the forest's growth. They find uses (such as chipboard) for small trees, so they can cut them sooner than if they waited for trees to grow big enough to make plywood or lumber. And they insist on cutting the rest of the lucrative old-growth forests for wood.

Now that the timber companies have cut down the trees on their own lands, there are too few big logs to feed the mills. This has led to cutthroat desperation as the mills scramble for timber and struggle to stay afloat. Virtually all remaining old growth is on public land. In the United States, this land is owned by the American people and managed by the U.S. Forest Service and the Bureau of Land Management. In Canada, the public forests are managed by the provincial government of British Columbia. Lumber com-

'HIGH-GRADING'

Loggers who don't think much about the future often cut the very best trees in a forest. Over time, that practice leaves the least desirable trees to pass on their traits to the next generation. In Korea, the Himalayas and the Mediterranean, centuries of this type of logging have degraded the gene pool. The only trees that survived the loggers' axes were the ones that were too crooked to make decent lumber.

panies are determined to keep their mills alive, so they press the agencies to let them log the public forests. But these lands are also major reservoirs of biological diversity, regulators of climate and sources of clean water, a wildlife habitat for dozens of species, as well as a source of recreation, education and scientific knowledge. These two conflicting goals – private industry profits on the one hand and the public's ecological interests on the other – set the stage for the political fight over the forest.

Political ecology

As long as the timber-company landowners had plenty of old-growth timber on their own property, they were happy for the Forest Service to sell little from the national forests, because it kept the price of wood from falling. But as they began to consume so much of their own forests to meet the demands of post-World War II housing, many companies changed their tune and turned to public lands to supply their mills. After World War II, the federal foresters abandoned their practice of culling individual trees from the forest. Clearcutting became the main style of logging in the national forests, regardless of the disruption of habitat, water quality and recreation it entailed. Between 1949 and 1970, the timber cut on the national forests more than doubled.

Ordered by Congress in 1976 to draw up new national forest plans to take these environmental factors into account, Forest Service planners aimed to reduce the cut by 20 percent. But these plans were nixed in the early 1980s by the Assistant Secretary of Agriculture in charge of the Forest Service, John Crowell. A Reagan appointee, Crowell came to the job from his post as general counsel of Louisiana-Pacific, which buys more timber from the agency than any other company. The plans went back for lengthy revisions but still recommended that 15 to 20 percent less timber be cut in western Washington, Oregon and California. The result satisfied nei-

JUNK BONDS MAKE FOR JUNK FORESTRY

It used to be that Northern California's Pacific Lumber Company was a timber operation that observers would point to as an example of good forestry. The family-run firm harvested selectively from its 195,000 acres of redwoods – including the largest holding of ancient redwoods outside of the state and national parks. Besides looking after the forest, Pacific Lumber looked after its own. Many employees lived in the company town of Scotia, the firm paid their kids' college tuition, and the company's measured pace of logging virtually guaranteed that the trees would last well into the next century. The firm had even made a handshake alliance with the Save-the-Redwoods League in 1920 and delayed logging on thousands of magnificent acres while the league raised funds to buy and preserve them.

All that changed in 1985, when Charles Hurwitz of the New York-based Maxxam Group bought the company and financed the takeover by issuing some $800 million in high-interest bonds. To pay the debt, Hurwitz doubled the rate of logging. His cash demands put an end to Pacific Lumber's practice of selective cutting. Since the late 1980s, huge tracts of land have been clearcut. Economically, the result has been a temporary logging boom which will be followed by the inevitable bust when the tall timber is gone. Ecologically, the logged land has been left denuded.

Maxxam has used Pacific Lumber and its priceless redwoods to finance its other takeovers, such as Kaiser Aluminum. What about environmental ethics? Hurwitz stated: "There's a story about the golden rule. Those who have the gold, rule."

ther industry nor the environmentalists. Both camps challenged nearly all the plans.

During the glacially slow planning process, heavy logging continued on federal forest lands in the Northwest. Even though the new Forest Service plans had yet to take effect, the agency recommended lower cuts. But every year, powerful congressional representatives from Northwest states used their leverage on influential committees to force the Forest Service to sell more timber than it had planned. On three major timber-producing forests in the Northwest, these increases ranged from 29 to 46 percent in 1987 alone.

Hope emerged, however, as conscientious staffers within the Forest Service began to speak out. In 1989, James Torrence, then regional forester in Oregon and Washington, called on politicians to respect the limits of the land's ability to produce. The Association of Forest Service Employees for Environmental Ethics (AFSEEE) sprang into being in 1989 to press the agency to be more responsive to ecological values. And in a remarkably candid 10-minute video, the forest supervisors of Alaska, Washington, Oregon and California put the agency's chief on notice in 1989 that they could not support politically motivated high logging levels. "The people who I am familiar with on the ground are not comfortable with this, and neither am I," warned Bob Devlin, supervisor of the Umpqua National Forest in Oregon. Under such conditions, he added, "I really can't be the steward of the public lands that you depend on me to be."

Keeping watch over the owl

Enter the northern spotted owl. First a lawsuit by a coalition of environmental groups pressured the federal government to protect the owl as a "threatened species." Then Congress directed a team of scientists from various federal agencies, headed by biologist Jack Ward Thomas, to draft a plan to safeguard the owl and bring it back from the brink of

SELLING OFF
THE TONGASS

The 16.9-million-acre Tongass National Forest is one of the wildest places in America, stretching along 600 miles of rugged coastline in the Alaska Panhandle. But its wildness is vanishing fast. Since the 1950s, two corporations with 50-year contracts to log in most of the Tongass have been paying bargain-basement prices for centuries-old trees. They pay as little as $15 for enough wood to build a house. Many trees are ground into pulp and shipped to Japan to make cellophane and disposable diapers. At these heavily subsidized prices, income from timber sales covers less than 10 percent of the Forest Service's costs. The federal government loses more than $40 million a year in the Tongass due to roadbuilding, planning and reforestation costs.

But there's more than money at stake here. The clearcutting of the Tongass destroys rich salmon streams and priceless habitat for grizzly bears and the Sitka black-tailed deer. Ninety percent of the salmon caught off southeastern Alaska were hatched in the Tongass. Ironically, with about 2,600 people employed in the fishing industry, more of the region's workers depend on salmon than on Tongass timber, which generates jobs for approximately 2,400 workers. Defenders of the timber industry claim that much of the Tongass is already protected as wilderness. But most of that is at high elevations – rocky outcroppings covered with ice and snow, not trees. Less than one-tenth of the rich, high-volume forests are protected so far. In October 1990, Congress passed a bill to eliminate some of the worst features of logging in the Tongass and to protect additional areas. But further reform is still needed. Conservationists are currently working to encourage legislation that would terminate two long-term timber contracts, which still assure a monopoly on Tongass timber extinction. The 1990 report proposed to set aside large tracts of the old-growth forest on which the owl depends and to reduce logging on federal lands to less than two-thirds of what it had been in the booming late 1980s. This was a bare minimum needed to ensure the survival of the owls. Even the authors of the Thomas report conceded that this minimal protection would reduce the owl population by 50 percent.

After the owl was officially listed as "threatened" under the Endangered Species Act, however, the federal government still tried to avoid putting the Thomas report into practice. The Bureau of Land Management attempted to substitute its own plan, which had little scientific basis, that would allow it to keep cutting in the crucial areas that link the proposed spotted owl areas.

The Bureau of Land Management is well known for looking at the forest as a marketable resource. Its forestlands in western Oregon total approximately 2.4 million acres and present a number of special problems. Under the terms of a 1937 act of Congress, these lands are managed primarily for timber production with minimal direction for environmental protection.

The Forest Service is not without its timber-first motives either. This federal agency devotes far more effort to timber production than to the other goals the law requires it to pursue. The Wilderness Society estimates that 75 percent of U. S. Forest Service activities are related directly or indirectly to logging or forest protection, including fire suppression. In fact, nearly half of the national forest supervisors complained in a 1989 memo that the timber program soaks up 35 percent of the agency's budget while fish, wildlife and recreation scrape by with 2 to 3 percent each. Some analysts point out that the Forest Service's timber focus justifies expenditures on programs such as road design and reforestation, which add to the agency's budget and staffing. The agency keeps a portion of timber receipts to fund its own activities, so, ironically, even wildlife biologists have a stake in timber sales. Economist

THE OWL IS A GOOD SIGN

The northern spotted owl, which depends upon large tracts of ancient forest for its survival, is threatened with extinction.

And when the owl population dwindles, it means something's wrong with the forest. This is why the U.S. Forest Service selected the owl as an indicator of the forest's health. Just as miners used canaries to indicate whether there was enough good air in a mine shaft, we can use the spotted owl to read the health of the forest.

The owl builds its nest in dead trees and preys on squirrels and other small mammals that eat the fruits of mycorrhizal fungi, spreading their spores. If the owl population falters, it may signal a drop in the population of those mammals, meaning that the fungi's spores are not being dispersed to young trees that need them.

What's more, the ancient forest is now so badly fragmented by logging that half the young owls born each year are killed by predators when the fledglings leave the nest in search of homes of their own.

So when the issue of the spotted owl is raised, remember – it's not just the owl but the whole forest that's at risk.

Randal O'Toole tells of one national forest biologist who advocated clearcuts as the best way to improve wildlife habitat, because the timber sales would add money to the forest's budget, allowing for improvements elsewhere in the forest.

Loggers share the owl's dilemma

The same trends that endanger the ancient forests also threaten the region's loggers and millworkers. These people are most directly affected by the fate of the forest, but they are not the ones who set its course. Forestry management decisions are made in San Francisco and Seattle, on Wall Street and Capitol Hill, while the human consequences are borne by working people. Timber has been the backbone of the region's economy for generations. But now that the old-growth forests are nearly exhausted, forest workers are concerned about the future. "I don't want unemployment – I want to work," says millworker Morgan after a three-month layoff. But the sad fact is that there simply is not enough timber to continue to employ him and all of his colleagues.

The basic problem for loggers is that the forest does not go on forever. A Spokane, Washington, activist summed up the situation in an interview with the *Oregonian*. "We're not up against the spotted owl," he said. "We're up against the Pacific Ocean." The forests just can't keep pace with the lumber companies' appetite for wood. As a result, the Forest Service is forecasting a drop of 1.5 billion board feet per year in logging on private lands by 1992. "As a society, we didn't recognize the limits of the resource," says ex-logger Atiyeh. "For instance, the North Santiam Valley could support two mills in perpetuity, not seven. So the spotted owl, the marbled murrelet and the old-growth logger are all endangered for the same reason – they're running out of habitat."

In desperation, woods workers and their families are demanding that the government continue supplying the lumber companies with timber from the national forests. But the

SPEAKING OUT FROM WITHIN

When U. S. Forest Service timber sale planner Jeff DeBonis moved from the Nez Percé National Forest in Idaho to Oregon's Willamette in 1988, it was like stepping back into the frontier era. "There were valleys on the Nez Percé forest that we stayed out of because of the accumulated effects of logging," he recalls. But in Oregon he found more extensively logged areas "that I was told to plan timber sales on."

DeBonis drafted a conference summary for his colleagues outlining the facts, criticizing the timber industry's stance and advocating a fundamental change in approach. "We, as an agency, are perceived by the conservation community as being an advocate of the timber industry's agenda," he wrote in January 1989. "Based on my 10 years with the Forest Service, I believe this charge is true." Two years later, he recalls, "I knew when I punched the button to send the memo that things wouldn't be the same."

Frustrated by the agency's reluctance to act, he circulated 300 flyers inviting dissident employees to join him in calling for change. The organization he founded – the Association of Forest Service Employees for Environmental Ethics (AFSEEE) – tapped into a well of discontent. Soon, his files bulged with responses. "My deepest congratulations on having the integrity to speak out and say what most all of us planners are thinking," one wrote.

THE CANADIAN CONNECTION

The situation in British Columbia is even worse than in the United States. The provincial government, which owns nearly all the forestland, seems more inclined to accommodate timber interests than act as stewards of the land. Every day, 1½ square miles of old-growth forest fall to the saw. Loggers are bound by fewer restrictions than in the United States, leading to such abominations as a 180-square-mile clearcut, plainly visible from outer space. Strathcona, a national park on Vancouver Island, is riddled with clearcuts and mines because lumber companies have been allowed to exchange land they owned for land with better timber in the middle of the publicly owned park. The province even lets timber companies manage some forests for decades at a time, using a system of tree-farm licenses, which practically amount to a gift of provincial forest to the company.

land simply cannot deliver on the inflated promises that politicians made to timber communities in the Northwest. In economics, as in nature, change is unavoidable. And change for these regions means developing an economy based on the forest's diversity of gifts, and not just on timber. Many parts of the Northwest have already made that transition, and now the remaining mill towns must do so as well.

Loss of timber supply isn't the only problem for the region's working people. From 1977 to 1988, lumber production in Oregon and Washington grew by 17 percent, from 11.5 to 13.5 billion board feet annually. So you might expect employment in the industry to have increased as well. But the number of workers in lumber and wood products actually fell by 19 percent, from 133,000 to 108,000. In other words, where it had taken 12 people to produce a million board feet per year, now it takes just eight. Automation is replacing timber-industry jobs as well. And this trend can be expected to continue, eliminating even more jobs.

Shipping jobs across the ocean

Another threat to the ancient forests is a cause that should have united millworkers and environmentalists long ago, and has just begun to do so. A staggering 24 percent of all the timber cut in Oregon and Washington in 1988 was shipped overseas as whole logs, mainly to Japan, Korea and China. This both depleted the forest and eliminated many jobs for residents of the Northwest who could have milled them locally. Many critics compare this to acting like a "banana republic," exporting raw materials and allowing other countries to reap the economic benefits of processing them into finished products. Even developing nations such as Thailand and Indonesia do not permit whole logs to leave their shores unmilled. If the billions of board feet of logs exported each year were milled at home instead of being shipped overseas, thousands of jobs could be saved, at least in the short run. This could stretch out the timber supply and give the region time to develop economic alternatives as logging declines.

Communities in transition

With one out of four logs cut in Oregon and Washington shipped unprocessed overseas, it is difficult for timber companies to support their claim that they have the workers' interests at heart. Their priority is profit, and if the logs bring 40 percent more money in Japan, onto the ship they go. It isn't the drive to save trees that is causing the economic transition in Northwest communities – it is the combination of overcutting, automation and log exports.

Old-growth timber bankrolled a good living for many of the region's people in return for hard, dangerous work. The timber industry has historically offered the best-paying jobs in mill towns. Timber workers are understandably reluctant to give up the standard of living they attained during the boom years of the late 1980s. No one wants to admit that the good times are over. But jobs that depend on the ancient forests are doomed, whether or not the last few groves are preserved. Exactly how soon they end matters a lot to loggers, who have their livelihoods to consider, but many of these jobs will be finished by the end of the decade, no matter what.

Financial insecurity has bred fear in many timber towns in the Northwest. But it's more than a financial issue, it's a cultural one. "This is what we do," says Harry Hershey, founder of Save Our Sawmills, a southern Oregon grassroots group. "We want to do it as long as we can, and we want our kids to do it." However, the way the forests have been depleted, this is a dream that can't come true. In Atiyeh's town, not a single member of the 1989 high-school graduating class entered the timber industry.

Ripe for change

Clearly, the present course of treating the earth's ancient forests as commodities to be consumed as fast as possible is a self-defeating practice that cannot be sustained. When forests are depleted, no one benefits. Right now, ecological integrity hangs in the balance, biodiversity is threatened, and families are worried about their futures. The situation is ripe for change, and in the next chapter, you'll see what can be done.

FOUR

PROTECTING OUR LEGACY

PROTECTING OUR LEGACY

How we can save our ancient forests

One of the most basic problems facing our forests is that people have started by asking the wrong question. We have asked what we need from the forest – such as profits, jobs, wood products and even recreation. As a result, we have taken more than the forest has to give. Now we need to change our way of thinking and begin by considering what the forest needs from us.

So much of the ancient forest has been logged, we must protect what little remains. Once that is done, we can consider sensible ways to draw timber from the rest of the forest – but only in ways that safeguard the integrity of the ecosystem. And finally, local communities can begin to make the inevitable transition away from an economy that depends almost exclusively on old-growth timber and toward a more diverse economy.

Protecting what remains

With nearly 90 percent of the ancient forests already gone from much of their range and many of them transformed into sterile tree plantations, we must act now to save what remains. A few old-growth forests have already been set aside as national parks or wilderness areas, but it takes more than isolated groves to support the myriad species that depend on this unique ecosystem. Most of the protected ancient forests are at high elevations, where the forest is less productive and therefore biologically not as rich. According to The Wilderness Society, just one-quarter of the remaining ancient forest is below 2,500 feet, and is in especially dire need of protection. And more than one-third of the remnant ancient forests are in stands so small, or so close to a road or clearing, that they do not provide suitable habitat for many old-growth dependent animals.

The destruction of the ancient forests makes their preservation an urgent issue. Less than 5 percent of the original ancient forest is protected. The rest is being logged at the rate of nearly 200,000 acres per year. In five of six national forests that The Wilderness Society studied in detail, the unprotected, unfragmented ancient forests will be gone by 1997 at current rates of logging and road building. On the sixth forest, the unprotected groves will be gone by the year 2010. The first order of business, then, must be to halt the logging of significant stands of ancient forest.

Halting the destruction

A cease-fire is needed, during which scientists can design an ecologically sound ancient forest preserve from the fragments of old-growth forest that remain. The preserve must be big enough to allow all native species that rely on old growth to continue to survive. And that means enough plants and animals of each kind that they are not all related to each other. The preserve should contain fragments close enough together to allow animals to migrate from one to another. Habitat corridors linking the fragments may provide a way for plants and animals to move between the old-growth patches. If any part of the preserve can't be linked to other fragments in this way, it

MILLENIUM GROVE, R.I.P.

People now working to save the ancient forests are waging a battle against time.

Although they may stave off logging in a grove temporarily, it might still be cut later. But once an ancient grove is logged to the ground, there's no going back.

Timber interests preyed on that disadvantage in the dramatic case of Millenium Grove, on the Willamette National Forest in western Oregon. On April 2, 1986, conservationists filed suit in the U.S. District Court seeking to stop Willamette Industries from destroying this 56-acre stand of trees that was thought to be as old as a thousand years and was estimated to be the largest grove of its age in Oregon. But on April 3, Willamette loggers ignored the pending legal action and cut down the entire grove. What took as long as 10 centuries to grow was destroyed in a single day.

The case of Millenium Grove lives on as a tragic example of the vulnerability of old-growth forests. Many existing forests face the same fate at the hands of the U.S. Forest Service, which proposes to log most of the remaining old-growth forests of the Pacific Northwest.

may need to be even larger to sustain itself. Finally, while this network is being designed, no ancient forests should be logged. If any are cut, they should be small stands that are too fragmented to provide healthy habitat.

Planning to protect these centuries-old forests means

thinking about the long term. The groves can't last forever – they will eventually fall prey to fire, disease or windstorms. As ecologist Elliott A. Norse points out, disturbances are bound to occur along some stands' path toward maturity. At least three acres of forestland must be set aside for each acre of ancient forest to be protected. It is not sufficient to protect just enough forest to keep an endangered species from becoming extinct because an extreme event could then push it over the edge. Protected forests need to be big enough to be resilient in the face of change, ensuring that new groves will be able to evolve from the old.

In addition, many ancient forests are too disconnected from their neighbors, or have areas that are too fragmented, for them to provide viable habitat over the long term. In those cases, ecologists must set aside some previously logged areas where in time, corridors of habitat can develop, linking one preserve with another. It may even be possible to practice ecological restoration in some of these groves, hastening by several decades the time when they attain the structure and function of old-growth stands.

Speaking up for the forests

Nearly all the remaining ancient forests are in the hands of the federal government and the province of British Columbia. Establishing these preserves in the United States will require an act of Congress, which can only pass if enough political pressure is brought to bear – and that means people who are willing to speak up for the forest. A bill to create a network of forest reserves was introduced by Rep. Jim Jontz (D-Ind.) in 1990 and garnered 131 co-sponsors. Although neither that bill nor a more moderate one reached the floor of the House during the 101st Congress, advocates of the ancient forests on Capitol Hill vowed to try again. Meanwhile, activists are fighting rear-guard actions to slow down the logging of the ancient forests while more permanent preservation is sought. Using tools that range from lawsuits to nonviolent blockades, people who care about the forests have halted numerous destructive timber sales while political battles played out.

The timber industry will still be able to continue, even after an ancient forest preserve is created. Setting aside this preserve would reduce the nation's timber supply only by a small fraction. Reasonable conservation measures could displace the need for much of the wood now being logged from ancient forest lands. All of the wood products we use can be made from younger trees, as long as at least some of them are grown slowly enough to yield high-quality wood.

Cutting trees, not forests

Setting aside the ancient forests is crucial, but it isn't enough. The other forests are important, too. The forest ecosystem and the rivers that run through it are affected by all of the forestland, not just the few ancient groves. So we must respect the ecosystem's needs outside the ancient forest preserve as well. Although it might seem at first that we should set aside the younger forests too, that isn't a practical answer. People in our society consume a lot of wood and wood products. Although this demand can be reduced, it will continue at some level. Even if we recycle all of our paper and use wood more wisely, we will still need to get pulp fiber and timber from somewhere. It's in our own interests to satisfy this demand in an ecologically sound manner – to improve the way in which wood is produced.

This is called "sustainable forestry" – forestry which puts nature ahead of timber and takes wood and other commodities from the forest at a rate that can be maintained indefinitely. This practice allows an astonishing array of forest life to persist despite the fact that some wood is being removed for human benefit. One promising idea is to surround a core area that is absolutely off-limits to logging with a ring of land where logging and human settlement are permitted, subject to

RETURNING THE LAND TO THE PEOPLE

In British Columbia, the movement to protect the ancient forests includes a large contingent of native peoples.

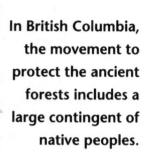

Few Native American tribes there signed treaties with the Canadian government, so they still claim millions of acres of their ancestral lands. After a long struggle, the Haida Nation in 1987 won the creation of a 350,000-acre park reserve on South Moresby Island off the northern coast of British Columbia, to be managed jointly for wilderness and traditional native uses. And the fight continues over 22,000-acre Meares Island, claimed by the native Clayoquot tribe, off the western coast of Vancouver Island. In 1984, a blockade by the Clayoquots and the local fishing fleet turned back a boatload of loggers who had come to cut the trees. The vigil to defend the island lasted for six months, when a court ruling prohibited further logging until the Clayoquots' claim to the land is settled.

tight restrictions that keep the ecosystem intact. Similar ideas have been tried with great success in New Jersey, where more than a million acres are set aside as the Pine Barrens preserve. The outer ring can still yield timber and other forest products but is held to a stricter standard than areas outside the reserve altogether.

Each forest is different. Forests vary depending on their elevation, soil, climate, the history of the site and other factors. A forester must listen to the land to determine what will be best at that spot. If we apply the lessons we learn by observing natural forests, we can reap a modest harvest of wood into the future.

Take no more than the forest offers. The level of logging on federal lands has been much higher than the forests could sustain for the long haul. Even the former regional forester for the Forest Service in Oregon and Washington has admitted that these rates cannot be maintained for the 10-year life of the new forest plans. One of the key meanings of sustainable is "able to be provided indefinitely." These levels of logging have no such future. A forest is like the fabled goose that laid golden eggs. It can only give so much so fast. Try to squeeze out more and you're bound to lose.

Federal timber sales must drop from their 1988 levels of more than 4 billion board feet in Oregon and Washington to no more than half that. The Wilderness Society estimates that some 2.3 billion board feet per year could be harvested in the long term. Other projections have ranged between 1 and 2 billion.

Good management replicates natural processes. Natural forests are the best model because they've proven they can sustain themselves for thousands of years. All forests need the natural cycles of growth, death, decay and regeneration. All are nurtured by the stages of succession that a natural forest experiences.

For example, practitioners of sustainable forestry see that the ecosystem thrives on "messiness" – logs, snags, uneven canopy and so on. They make sure those elements remain in a forest after logging to offer hiding places for rodents, nurse logs for

IN THE WILD IRIS FOREST

One warm May afternoon, Jan Iris drove the author and his high-school ecology students to a beautiful, park-like spot. They clambered off his flatbed truck amid 60- to 100-foot-tall trees and made camp in a small clearing. Only the next morning, on a tour of Iris' operation, did they learn that he had logged the area two years before. They could hardly believe that this inviting spot had been logged so recently until they saw the stumps, nearly flush to the ground. He had taken many trees for lumber and firewood, but left the forest standing.

Wild Iris Forestry, founded by Iris and his wife, Peggy, on the north coast of California, manages 2,000 acres logged in the 1950s and '60s. Broadleaf trees have sprouted on the land, with some Douglas fir mixed in. Larger timber companies frequently ignore hardwood forests such as this. If they do log there, they reduce the trees to pulp and plant uniform farms of Douglas fir.

Instead, Iris lives on what the forest has to offer. He ponders each cut carefully, considering how a tree's removal would benefit the forest. He allows the best trees to keep growing to improve the forest and leaves many specimens, especially madrones, for aesthetic value.

Iris saws the logs on a mobile mill that he tows into the forest, using narrow lanes just big enough for a flatbed truck. He also cures and kilns the lumber, sometimes processing it into flooring, and sometimes selling it to cabinet makers. His wood fetches a high price, about three to four times higher than that of industrial mills.

seedlings, and moist rotting wood for fungi and termites. If their logging creates a clearing, they try to mimic the size and shape of patches that natural processes open up in a forest. Or sometimes they take trees singly or in small clumps, because small disturbances like that are common to a natural forest as well.

The "greenprint" for forestry is to be found in all of the native, unmanaged forests, no matter what their age. An ancient forest tells us how the ecosystem works in a 400-year-old forest; to learn about younger stands, we must look to those that grew up after more recent upheavals, such as the Yacolt forest fire of 1902 in Washington and Oregon, or the 1921 blowdown on the Olympic Peninsula. These natural forests are our teachers.

Cultivate diversity. The forest feeds on many kinds of diversity – of age, species and habitat. Sustainable forestry welcomes and even encourages this diversity, instead of extinguishing it as is done in tree plantations. As described in Chapter 3, forests made up of a variety of species and ages are more resistant to pests and disease. These diverse stands are also likely to support the very predators that can keep those pests in check through a system of natural controls.

Every species matters. Researchers have recently come to understand the value of tree species besides the commercially valuable Douglas fir. Timber managers who try to eradicate "competing plants" and other organisms can kill off vital elements that are needed for the health of the forest, effectively shooting themselves in the root, as it were.

Foresters have tried to cultivate diversity in two ways. Some have avoided establishing stands of trees that are all the same age, as they would be after clearcutting or similar logging (see p. 71). They concede that clearcuts can be useful in some circumstances (such as removing a diseased stand) but argue that the technique is vastly overused. They prefer an alternative – known as "selection," "all-aged" or "uneven-aged" management – cutting trees singly or in small groups. The result is

THE 'NEW FORESTRY'

Forest Service ecologist Tom Atzet pulls off a gravel road, gets out and points toward Chinaman Hat, a 3,500-foot peak in the Siskiyou Mountains. The hillside is covered in a grey stubble of trees killed in a 1987 fire. On the mountain behind, the stubble is broken by a swath of green trees. Under the Forest Service's usual practices, all the trees would have been cut. Instead, many snags and trees were left. Atzet explains that this is a trial run of a logging technique that may be used even in unburned areas. New Forestry, brainchild of ancient-forest scientist Jerry Franklin and his colleagues, tries to imitate the state of a forest after a moderate fire. Fire rarely kills all the trees in a grove; a few trees of various sizes, species and ages are usually spared. Similarly, under New Forestry practices, several live trees per acre remain when an area is logged. Most large snags stay and logs are left strewn across the ground. These practices are aimed at leaving a "biological legacy" to shelter wildlife and speed the renewal of the forest. Although New Forestry is still in the experimental stages, several national forests – including the Siskiyou and Willamette in Oregon – have already decided to use this approach on tens of thousands of acres.

New Forestry attempts to get the most ecological benefit from logged areas – as Franklin has said, "to share the sandbox." On second-growth forests, where continued logging is appropriate, it may be valuable. But environmentalists caution that this so-called "kinder and gentler forestry" cannot substitute for ancient forest protection and should not be used to justify further old-growth logging.

a stand that ranges from centuries-old through middle-aged (50 to 100 years) to young poles, saplings and seedlings.

Other foresters view diversity on a landscape scale and believe that some parts of the landscape must be maintained in each stage of forest succession, so the animals that inhabit that stage will have somewhere to live and eat. A forest is like a human community, they observe, where a healthy population includes every age group from infants to old people, not just children and teen-agers as is the case in a plantation. In the final analysis, both kinds of diversity may prove to be important.

Movement has begun

Thanks to the groundswell of demands in the late 1980s for better forest management, some progress toward sustainable forestry is already occurring. Attempts at less destructive logging have arisen all over the Northwest, goaded by a public that is increasingly outraged at the abuses the land has suffered.

Even the Forest Service bureaucracy has begun to move. A program called New Perspectives was launched in 1990 with great fanfare, aimed at giving greater consideration to forest ecology in managing the forests. Experiments in New Forestry (see page 67) are planned for several national forests in Oregon and Washington.

Elsewhere, some agency officials took action on their own. Forest Supervisor Tom Kovalicky of the Nez Percé National Forest in Idaho has put fish, wildlife and recreation on a par with timber in deciding how to manage the forest, and has won praise from conservationists for his stance. District Ranger John Berry of the Mt. Hood National Forest attended a seminar on uneven-aged management and decided to drastically reduce clearcutting on his ranger district.

Progress isn't confined to the Forest Service. The 300,000 acre Olympic Experimental State Forest in western Washington is in the process of banishing tree farming and launching a full-blown test of New Forestry. Besides preserving the great major-

SHUTTING THE COURTHOUSE DOORS

Environmental laws have offered the most effective defense in the campaign to protect the last remaining ancient forests.

These laws – such as the Endangered Species Act, the National Environmental Policy Act, the Migratory Bird Act and the National Forest Management Act – have allowed concerned citizens to insist that the Bureau of Land Management and the Forest Service obey the law. Some of the worst abuses of the land have been stopped as a result of suits brought in the federal courts by these citizen groups.

But powerful Northwest lawmakers have successfully persuaded Congress in the past to insulate the Forest Service and the Bureau of Land Management from these suits – in effect, granting the agencies immunity from public action in the courts. Such bans were enacted every year between 1984 and 1989. By locking the courthouse doors to citizens, heavy logging of vital ancient forests has gone unchecked.

Whatever resolution is reached in Congress for protecting the ancient forests, legal remedies must remain open in case the federal agencies fail to carry out the law. It's the American way.

ity of the tract's 17,000 acres of ancient forest, the new plan aspires to both produce timber and protect ecological values throughout the entire forest. New Perspectives and New Forestry are still in the experimental stage and are thus unproven as methods of maintaining biodiversity and ecological balance. Nonetheless, they are encouraging signs that the forestry profession is beginning to look at new ways of doing business.

The Bureau of Land Management lags behind, however. The existing management plans for the Bureau's districts in western Oregon were prepared approximately 10 years ago and call for very high annual rates of logging. These plans are overdue for revision, but new plans are unlikely to be ready until 1993 at the earliest. Meanwhile, the agency proposes to sell timber at a rate that is 70 percent higher than the amount recommended to give adequate protection to the threatened northern spotted owl.

Public lands are not the only areas where management is an issue. Many small landowners have been put off from harvesting timber on their land because they care more about aesthetics and wildlife than about income or wood production. Sustainable forestry may be the only way they will allow chainsaws on their land to help offset the imminent decline of timber from industry's holdings and national forests. Even on industrial lands, the public has a legitimate interest in how forestry is practiced, because it affects many public resources, such as water quality downstream and wildlife populations. Just as building codes and zoning ordinances set limits on how people may use their private property, so too can forest-practice laws enforce basic good forestry.

A few companies, such as Collins-Pine in northeastern California, are already doing a good job. This timber firm, which has logged selectively in its 87,000 acres of pine and fir forest for the last 50 years, is unusual in that its land and mill are owned by separate entities. The foresters decide how much logging the forest can tolerate and spare the most vigorous trees to extend the harvest.

California has taken the lead in requiring certain basic forest practices – such as unlogged buffer strips around streams, less harmful logging methods on steep slopes and smaller

A CLEARCUT BY ANY OTHER NAME

Once clearcutting got a bad name, foresters came up with new terminology to disguise their damaging logging practices.

"Regeneration cut" is a term frequently used in place of clearcut. "Shelterwood" and "seed tree" logging are techniques that vary only slightly from clearcutting and have virtually the same effect. With these methods, loggers cut all the trees on a site, although they do it over several years and two or three episodes. As in a clearcut, the trees are replaced with a stand of new trees, all the same age. Shelterwood and seed tree logging methods may not result in areas as unsightly as clearcuts, but they can be even more damaging, since they're often used to circumvent limits on the size of clearcuts.

clearcuts. However, the regulations in most of the state still don't go far enough. Voters in 1990 turned down an initiative that would have banned clearcuts and stopped the timber companies from overcutting their land. The central coast of California has a stricter set of rules, however, that has kept the forest intact even as its timber is harvested. These "Santa Cruz rules" ban clearcutting, allow the timber companies to harvest no more than once per decade on any site and impose tough standards to control erosion and preserve soil fertility. One forester in the area, Mike Jani of Big Creek Lumber Co., calls this "pretty forestry" and praises it for keeping the "environ-

TEAHOUSE OF THE OREGON MILL OWNER

Enterprising businesses have already begun to take the value of wood products into account in the Northwest, such as the Oregon mill owner who started cutting wood to the metric dimensions common in Japan. He built a Japanese teahouse at his mill to attract buyers and gained millions in lumber sales to that country.

mental monkey off our backs." Big Creek's crews log with such care that erosion, which is usually aggravated by logging, actually declines after many of Big Creek's harvests.

What about people?

These are times of wrenching transition for many in the forest communities of the Northwest, brought on by overcutting, automation and log exports. Dozens of communities in the Pacific Northwest owe their existence to the timber industry. A Forest Service study shows that even without stricter environmental controls, the number of timber-related jobs in the Douglas-fir region of Washington and Oregon would drop to just over half of its 1970 level by the year 2000, from 119,000 to 64,000. The jobs that the industry claims will be lost because of the spotted owl pale next to this decline.

The inescapable reality, says ex-logger George Atiyeh, is that "if you base your economy on the extraction of a natural resource, eventually it comes to an end." The people in these communities want to stay there and make an honorable living, but the timber industry will employ fewer of them. The vital relationship between the land and the people who live near the forest needs to be restored so that men and women can reap the benefits of the ecosystem without exploiting it. A future can be built on all of the forest's values, including its renewable resources, and on the intelligent development of new sources of economic support. The people of this region can make the necessary transition, but they will need the support of industry, government and cooperative community organization to do it.

The future of forestry. Sustainable forestry offers the people who live around the forest a positive role that benefits them as well as the ecology of the forest. The new forms of forestry described here would actually require more labor to produce a given amount of lumber. Over the last three decades, the timber industry has continued to automate. In contrast, sustainable forestry requires the labor of skilled workers. So far, however, it has paid lower wages than logging in the ancient forests because the abundance of old-growth trees has kept the price of wood low.

The current price of wood reflects the cost of extracting a tree from the ancient forests, not the cost of replacing it by growing a new tree in its place. As an indication of this, the countries that buy logs from the Pacific Coast – primarily Japan, China and Korea – exhausted their ancient forests long ago. They now value wood quite highly and therefore bid much higher prices for timber than Americans do. Port Orford cedar, once favored by Americans for making arrow shafts, is unavailable in the United States because it commands such high prices from Japanese builders.

As the North American old growth runs out, or is set off-limits, the price of wood will rise here, too. When that occurs, timber will be valued highly enough to warrant competitive wages for the labor-intensive methods of sustainable forestry.

Getting the greatest value from each log. As the raw material becomes scarcer, efforts should be made to generate more jobs per tree. That means not exporting logs or cants (roughly cut logs). Instead, people in forest communities can devise ways of creating more finished wood products before the wood leaves the region. Lumber brings higher prices than logs, flooring more than lumber, and furniture higher prices still. Doors, cabinets, windows, frames and moldings can all be made in timber-dependent communities.

Sustainable land practices will fit in with these economically sound moves by improving lumber quality. Wood from slower-grown trees has tighter-spaced rings, which makes it both stronger and more beautiful. It also contains less of the warp-prone juvenile wood. Good forestry can yield boards that nearly replicate the fine timber of old-growth trees, thus making the wood more attractive to process into valuable products.

Respecting the workers. In the independent, self-reliant culture of loggers and millworkers, self-determination is valued even more than outside help, and timber workers already have a lot of valuable skills. Atiyeh ticks off the jobs on a logging team: the rigging slinger, who knows how to supervise a crew; the people who operate the heavy machinery – "the ability to become one with a piece of equipment is a very salable skill." Other positions, such as that of choker-setter (requiring a person to clamber through the brush wrapping cables around logs) are not jobs that anyone stays in for very long.

"The guy who's the most endangered," Atiyeh concludes, "is the guy who owns the logging company." Most of his wealth is tied up in logging equipment, its value declining as the need for old-growth logging machinery disappears.

Now is the time for communities in the region to begin to participate in the transition instead of being buffeted by it. Legislation can help by giving residents the tools they need to pursue a future with a future. Congress and the states can provide resources for local people to consider the possibilities and determine which ones make sense for them. Residents will be able to exercise this self-determination more effectively if the government opens more doors for them with measures such as educational and training programs (as the GI bill did for veterans) and low-interest start-up loans for new businesses.

Some observers have put a lot of faith in tourism as a wellspring of economic growth. But many residents are concerned that tourist dollars will affect them in unwelcome ways, providing only low-wage jobs and high-cost housing.

Studies of how communities can make effective transitions to more stable economies, such as the research now being conducted by The Wilderness Society, can help to provide vital facts and strategies.

Looking at the big picture. Among the region's great assets are its clean air and water and the open spaces so near its population centers. These much sought-after values have fueled the region's economic growth in recent years, coupled with the fact that wages run about 15 percent below the national average because of the lower cost of living. The timber industry now accounts for less than 6 percent of Oregon's economy, and even less in Washington. Yet the region's beauty and livability depend on the forest, which provides the clean water, verdant vistas and outdoor opportunities that have attracted new businesses and sustained existing ones. It would be foolish to compromise these lasting qualities to perpetuate the doomed old-growth boom for a few more years.

Seeing new crops in the forest. Entrepreneurs recognize other products in the forest besides timber. Orville Camp brags of the ubiquitous huckleberries that grow on logged land like his own and can be sold for $15 a gallon. A sign on one hardware store in western Oregon proclaims that the proprietors buy the bark of the cascara tree (used as a laxative) which they sell to pharmaceutical companies. Markets exist and are expanding for the gourmet mushrooms and truffles found in the forest, and for products such as western red cedar leaf and the pearly everlasting, both used in floral arrangements. Like sustainable forestry, this approach can increase the residents' connection to the cycles that go on in the forest and give them a greater stake in its survival.

Defining new missions. Now that so much effort has been spent on the destruction of the forest environment, the talent of many of the same people is needed to help it heal. Former Forest Service dissident Jeff DeBonis urges the agency to redefine its task to encompass restoration of forest ecosystems and providing advice to private landowners on taking good care of their forests. Another federal agency – the National Park Service – has already pioneered this approach with its efforts to rehabilitate 36,000 acres of logged land that it added to Redwood National Park in 1978. This turnabout would suit some logging contractors just fine. One bulldozer operator was hired by the park to help remove some of the roads that he had put in for the timber companies when they owned the land. Conservationist Lou Gold tells of talking with the contractor who was building the road Gold was trying to stop near the Kalmiopsis Wilderness. The contractor explained that he gives money to environmental groups and that his favorite charity is creating nature trails that are accessible to the handicapped. "But I've got to pay for my $10 million of equipment. Why can't I get a contract to take out a road?"

How to make it happen

Once we have decided what kind of relationship with the forest we wish to cultivate, the issue remains how to make it happen. It's often tougher to implement a solution than to arrive at one. Here are several models of how to transform forestry:

Bonding with the land. In his book *Tree Talk*, Ray Raphael suggests a novel arrangement he calls "stewardship." The basic premise: to give a small partnership the long-term responsibility for a section of the forest, subject to guidelines that would prevent the abuses that occur with tree-farm licenses in British Columbia. The people managing the forest would have a lasting connection to the land, instead of being posted there on their way up a career ladder. They'd be rewarded for improving the land's condition and productivity, not for harvesting its wood. A similar system has been in place for decades in Switzerland, which is where Raphael got the idea.

The Forest Service has already tried "stewardship contracts" with some of its tree planters, who are paid not just for the number of trees they plant, but also on the basis of how many are alive after three years. That provides the planters with an incentive to do a high-quality planting job.

Stewardship systems are a way for the rules of the game to reflect the reciprocal relationship between forests and humans. The system can be set up so that people are rewarded for a healthy forest with all of its cycles and species intact. Ultimately, people will benefit from this healthy forest as well.

'If the incentives lead, the bureaucrats will follow.' That's the controversial perspective of Randal O'Toole, an Oregon economist. He argues that agency staffers do what they're rewarded for doing. Under the current system, that means selling timber. The agency keeps part of the sale price to fund other activities – such as road building, campgrounds and wildlife habitat projects. But none of these other programs bring in revenue. O'Toole's idea is to allow the U.S. Forest Service to charge for recreational use of the national forests, giving the agency a financial stake in preserving ancient forests. Money from wilderness users would go to expand wilderness and wild river areas. Fees from developed recreation would support campgrounds, and so on. A portion of all agency revenues would go into a fund to protect biological diversity, which benefits everyone.

O'Toole estimates that wilderness use would cost about $5 a day and other parts of the forest, such as picnic areas, about $3. He envisions steeper fees for more heavily used wilderness areas to reduce crowding in the popular ones.

Critics of O'Toole's proposal point out that such fees dis-

THE ANCIENT FOREST ALLIANCE

In an effort to save our ancient forests, a coalition of national and regional groups representing millions of Americans across the United States has banded together, calling themselves the Ancient Forest Alliance.

The Alliance is urging Congress to pass legislation that will protect old growth and the plants and animals that help make it unique – including the spotted owl, marbled murrelet, Pacific yew and fisher. The Alliance is also working to ensure that the legislation includes economic assistance for the region's communities. Immediate protection of ancient forests, however, rests with reform of the U.S. Forest Service and Bureau of Land Management, and a halt to the overzealous logging of our national forests.

Working towards these common goals, the Ancient Forest Alliance meets with high-level White House officials, testifies before Congress, goes to court to enforce environmental protection for the ancient forests, educates the public, provides technical information to federal agencies, and works with the scientific community to learn more about our ancient forest resource.

criminate against the poor, that free access to the wilderness should be everyone's prerogative and that this system alone will not suffice to protect the ancient forests. The Wilderness Society opposes any fees for wilderness use.

The thorny issues surrounding O'Toole's proposal illustrate the complexity of the problem.

In search of common ground. Forestry is more than just a matter of money; it's a matter of politics and fiercely held convictions. Amid the pitched battles that have been fought over legislation to preserve forestland or offer it for logging, opposing sides have sometimes been able to negotiate their differences. Loggers, miners and environmentalists in Montana's Kootenai National Forest reached a pact in 1990 on how much land should be set aside as wilderness and how much released for logging and mining.

Even more dramatically, forest practices on state and private lands in Washington are controlled through a treaty between environmentalists, the timber industry, Native Americans and the state government. The negotiations began in 1986 after an encounter between the head of an industry trade association and an Indian leader. "It was driven by their frustration at the way things were going," recalls Bill Jacobs of the Washington Forest Protective Association. "In any fight, nobody really won, or if somebody did win, someone else lost. They realized there had to be a better way."

The four sides embarked on a voyage of a hundred meetings to hammer out the Timber, Fish and Wildlife Agreement – including stream-side protections, logging methods, road standards and so on. Besides gaining stiffer protections for the forest, the environmentalists within this association were able to visit industry land and see what was happening in the field, giving them an opportunity to respond early to logging plans. The industry, in turn, gained some certainty about logging rules. In late 1990, as the agreement's original term ran out, talks broke down. Although such delicate arrangements are often fraught with potential conflicts, they also provide useful tools for problem solving that can benefit everyone.

A lasting resolution to the issues raised here requires the participation of a broad base of interested parties, from the loggers who have worked in the forests for 20 years to the campers and bird watchers who frequent it. The ultimate goal, though it may not be easily attainable, is a consensus shaped by everyone with a stake in the forest – which means all of us.

Moving ahead on all fronts

All of these issues – protecting the forests, reducing timber sales and exports, creating more intelligently managed forests and helping local people develop more diverse economies – will require effort to bring them about. We also need to begin to adjust to a world in which wood and paper are scarcer and more valuable than they now seem to be. Legislation is the surest way to preserve ancient forests on public lands. The rules of the game need to change, and we, as interested citizens, can help make it happen in a variety of ways. In the next chapter, you'll see what you can do to help realize these visions.

FIVE

BECOMING PART OF THE SOLUTION

BECOMING PART OF THE SOLUTION

What you can do to help save our ancient forests

The fate of the ancient forests is in our hands for several reasons. First, trees are logged to satisfy a demand for lumber and paper products. As consumers, we can help lower this demand by making responsible choices in the course of our daily lives. Second, the governments of the United States and British Columbia are the stewards of much of the remaining ancient forests. As citizens, we can influence how our forests are treated by communicating our views to our elected representatives and building a movement toward forest protection. Finally, we can visit the forests and build relationships with them as places of inspiration, recreation or even livelihood, ties that will strengthen whatever other actions we take to protect them.

Some signs of reform are emerging in the way forests are treated, but we still have a long way to go. By staying abreast of the issues and keeping up the pressure, we can help implement major changes that will protect the forests from further destruction. Action is needed at all levels, and no effort is too small. So, take your pick from the following ideas, and choose the ancient forest action that most appeals to you.

Conscious consumption

The policies suggested in the previous chapter, particularly preserving the remaining ancient forests, would reduce the supply of old-growth lumber from western North America. If we were to continue to use the same amount of wood, more trees would have to be harvested somewhere else, making other forests suffer the consequences of our demands. The more logical solution, and the only viable one, is to learn to live within our means. Because old-growth lumber accounts for only a small fraction of total wood consumption in the United States, this shouldn't be too hard to do. We can, and must, reduce our demand for wood to make up for the ancient forests we want to save.

Many simple measures can be taken that could have a major effect on the demand for timber without significantly affecting our lifestyles. We'll start with the easiest things first.

Reduce, reuse, recycle. Everyone knows that recycling paper saves trees – as many as 13 trees per ton of paper recycled. This statistic does not refer to the majestic giants of the ancient forests, but rather the smaller pines and poplars of plantations grown in the southern United States specifically for paper production. Magnificent 400-year-old trees aren't usually turned into pulp (except in Alaska's Tongass National Forest), just as steers are not ground entirely into hamburger. Instead, the best, soundest parts of old-growth trees are made into lumber and plywood (the steaks of the wood business), while the sawdust and edges are used for particleboard, chipboard and pulp.

But there is a connection. When you recycle paper or simply make do with less, you reduce the demand, making it possible to use smaller trees for lumber, rather than cutting the old growth for this purpose and using the younger trees for pulp. One Forest Service researcher has shown that an increase in the recycled content of American paper of only 10 percent would allow lumber use to grow while timber harvest declines. The trees that would otherwise be pulped into paper could either be sawn into 2x4s or chipped to make chipboard (a substitute for plywood, one-third of which comes from the Pacific Northwest). If less forestland is needed to grow small trees for chipping and pulping, other trees can be grown longer to provide larger lumber and plywood, reducing the incentive to cut trees from the ancient forests and neighboring groves for these products. As an added bonus, recycling saves scarce landfill space and cuts down the pollution generated in paper manufacture.

We can take a leaf from the forest and behave the way it does – establishing cycles that use materials over and over. Here are a few things you can do:

• Use less paper when possible. Bring grocery bags back to the supermarket to fill with another load of food (some supermarkets offer refund incentives for this). Better yet, bring your own cloth shopping bag for short trips to the market and a folding cart with a box for larger loads. Use cloth rags and sponges instead of paper towels for cleaning, cloth instead of paper napkins at the table.

• Write or photocopy on both sides of the paper you use; use blank back sides for scratch paper or cut them up and staple them together to make notepads.

• Save your wastepaper and get it into the hands of local recyclers. Check your Yellow Pages under "Recycling" or "Waste Paper." Call your recycling center or garbage company to find out which kinds of paper they accept, and how they collect it – typically at recycling centers, at the curbside with your trash or in boxes provided by local charities. Start a recycling habit at work, at your child's school, church, temple or club.

• Request that merchants take you off their "junk mail" lists, helping to remove tons of paper from circulation before it reaches your circular file. Share catalogues and magazine subscriptions with your friends.

• Buy recycled paper goods. Now that people have begun recycling in earnest, paper companies need to make "previously owned paper" into new products. To do that, a demand for recycled paper must exist. The good news: everything from toilet paper to high-quality writing paper and birthday cards are now available in recycled paper products.

• Buy in bulk. Less packaging saves money as well as paper.

• Support businesses that take action to reduce their use of paper – cutting their use of throwaway products in general, not just substituting plastic for paper. Do the same in your workplace. And when you buy a coffee or soda to go, it's great if you can bring your own mug or reusable cup instead of getting a disposable paper container.

• Treat your baby to the comfort and economy of cloth diapers instead of disposables. On the Tongass National Forest, many ancient trees are turned into pulp. Says Bart Koehler of the Southeast Alaska Conservation Council, "When a 400-year-old tree ends up on some baby's bottom, that's an insult to all that's good and right with the world."

Get the most out of each board. North Americans consume more lumber per person than the inhabitants of any other region on earth – about 1,000 board feet per year, on average, for a family of four. That's enough wood to build a chest-high fence three-quarters of an inch thick, as long as a football field – neck high, if you include plywood. Some of that wood is used wisely, but a lot of it goes to waste or is discarded before its usefulness is exhausted. North America is the only continent where wood is so inexpensive. How many times have you passed by a house that was being renovated, and seen perfectly good boards in the dumpster? Now that the old-growth forests are nearly gone, we need to adjust to the fact that we aren't on the frontier anymore. Here are some things you can do to make better use of our precious natural resources:

• Use recycled lumber where possible. Some businesses specialize in reselling the sound wood from demolished buildings. These boards are as functional as new wood, and have the character that comes with years of use. Michael Evanson, a used-lumber broker on the northern California coast, used to pick through the wreckage of torn-down buildings and salvage perhaps a quarter of the wood. Now he's dismantling a collection of sheds board by board and recovering 90 percent of the wood – a method made economically feasible by the increasing price and scarcity of old-growth redwood lumber. Look under "Salvage Merchandise" in the Yellow Pages.

• Recycle your scrap wood, too. The Seattle Solid Waste Utility, for one, has more than 14 different projects to reduce and recycle trash, including the recycling of scrap lumber and wood at Seattle's Transfer Stations. Find out how your city can do the same.

• Design before you buy. The better you think through a project in advance, the less wood you'll probably waste. But over-designing is common and a lot of Saturday carpenters overbuild, just to be safe. When was the last time something came close to breaking because you used a 2x4 instead of a 2x6? There's an elegance to building with just the right amount of material.

• Reuse wood around your house. Studs from the inside wall you remove may be perfectly good in the fence you're planning to build next summer. Sure, it takes a few minutes to remove the nails. But it takes 70 to 100 years to grow a good lumber tree.

Be a wily wood buyer. Lumber production affects the forest very differently, depending on how the trees were grown and logged. Armed with a little knowledge, you can avoid lumber that was made by destroying ancient forests. And just by asking, you can raise the issue to wood professionals who might not have thought much about it before.

• Ask around. When you go to a lumberyard or homeowners' supply store, try to find out whether the wood on sale came from the ancient forests. Your question will convey your concern to the people in charge. Just a handful of people asking about the origin of their lumber is enough to catch the attention of the store managers. Most lumber with large cross-sections (more than 10 inches in any direction) comes from old-growth forests. Often, you can laminate a handful of second-growth boards

together to take the place of a beam cut from an old-growth log.
• Boycott old-growth redwood. For the time being, all old-growth redwood is cut from ancient forests. (Recycled boards were cut there, too, but that damage has already been done.) If the rings in the board are so narrow and tightly spaced that it's hard to count them, you are probably looking at an old-growth board.
• Look for the good forest-keeping seal of approval. As of late 1990, responsible foresters and environmental activists were collaborating on a program to certify lumber as sustainably grown and harvested if it met certain criteria. By late 1991, this should already be in place in part of California. Sustainably produced lumber will be labeled PCEFP: Pacific Certified Ecological Forest Products.

Gimme shelter. In the United States, more than 60 percent of lumber and 75 percent of plywood goes to build and remodel homes and offices. North America is one of the few places in the world where such a large percentage of homes are built of wood. Our obsession with lumber as a building material is rooted deep in our frontier culture. In the mid-19th century, when pioneering American settlers first arrived in San Diego, they found a town that was constructed entirely of adobe, a locally available, ecologically sound material made of sun-dried clay and straw. They said, in effect, "Hell no, we're not living in mud huts," and began to bring in lumber. Wooden houses have been erected all over the country – even on the Great Plains and in the deserts of the Southwest, hundreds of miles from the nearest timber trees.

Americans prize wooden homes highly. But the forests can no longer afford us that luxury. In fact, even before the courts ordered the protection of the spotted owl, the Forest Service was already predicting a 14-percent drop in lumber production in California, Oregon and Washington by the year 2000. We need to consider ways to obtain the same shelter and housing without using as much wood. Here are two possibilities:

• Reframe your thinking. If you're in the construction trade or have occasion to build your own house, check into timber-frame construction or a method called "truss framing." These building techniques produce better buildings, use less wood and create more jobs. (See page 89.)

• Venture beyond wood. Wood is far from the only workable construction material. It makes the most ecological sense to build from what's locally available: brick in the Northeast and Midwest, adobe in the Southwest, concrete block wherever there's gravel and sand (and no earthquake hazards). Rammed earth, a mixture of soil and a little cement, is a versatile material and can be used virtually anywhere.

When there's less wood on the market and it costs more, at least one of these alternatives will probably be right for you. Wood is worth using when it can be showcased in all of its beauty – not simply tucked away as a stud inside a wall.

Good for more than just timber. There's a growing movement in the Pacific Northwest to market goods besides timber that can be gathered from the forest. A number of communities are using flowers, fungi, berries or tree bark from the forest to replace part of the income they are losing as the timber industry declines. They collect cones for wreaths, Oregon grapes as an herbal remedy, cedar bark for potpourris and wild mushrooms for the gourmet market. Mushroom hunting actually became so popular that Six Rivers National Forest banned commercial harvest of them for fear it would disrupt the fungi's ability to reproduce. (Moderation is important when taking anything from nature.) See the Natural Resources section to learn how to get more information on these products.

Send a clear message

Part of the problem with how the forests have been treated is that the people in charge, timber executives and agency officials, think that the public's ancient forests belong to them.

SMART FRAMING

Most wood-frame houses in the United States are built with what is called "stick framing," in which the walls hold up the roof and the upper floors. The walls are built of 2x4s, spaced every 16 inches, or 2x6s, spaced every 24 inches. Other framing members, such as joists and rafters, must be 2x8, 2x10 or even 2x12. These methods, which require a lot of wood and relatively little skill or advance planning, are ways of substituting wood for know-how.

A better method, called timber-frame construction, which is employed extensively in Europe, uses posts and beams from which the house is hung. This allows much greater flexibility in choosing the materials for the walls, and allows them to be less muscular, because they no longer need to bear any weight. Timber framing requires less material and more labor, which could also be an advantage in these times when resources and jobs have both become scarce. Houses built with this method last longer than the average, hastily constructed tract home. "Turning old-growth into dingbats is a waste," says George Atiyeh. "Sell it to the Timber Framers Guild and they'll build a house that'll last as long as it took the trees to grow."

Another possibility is called "truss framing," which uses smart engineering techniques to distribute the stresses that the house bears (weight, wind, seismic waves) to all the other parts of the building. This type of framing uses 20 to 30 percent less wood than a conventional house, and can be built entirely with 2x4s.

They don't. These magnificent forests are the heritage of us all. As you come to know and care about these forests, and to realize how far off the mark the conduct of our government officials has been, you need to make your opinions known to them. You elect them, pay them through your taxes and have the right to demand that they represent your views.

To get you started, The Wilderness Society has a Citizen's Action Kit which includes preprinted postcards to elected and appointed officials. To order your kit, send a check or money order for $2.00 to the Wilderness Society, 900 17th St. N.W., Washington, DC 20006.

Besides the federal agencies (the U.S. Forest Service and the Bureau of Land Management), state governments in Washington and Oregon and the provincial government in British Columbia control large tracts of forestland. Even the forest that the timber industry owns is rightly of concern to all of us. Salamanders and owls can't read "No Trespassing" signs. And salmon migrate up streams that run through land owned by corporations, private individuals and public agencies alike. Private property rights are not absolute. The citizenry has the right to control how individuals use their land if it affects the common good. The Endangered Species Act, for example, regulates the use of lands in ways that may affect endangered or threatened species. From British Columbia south to California, the state and provincial governments make rules regulating the forest practices that private industry may employ. In addition, the executives of timber companies need to hear how you feel.

Here are some important issues and the people who are responsible for effecting the laws and practices concerning them.

End log exports. This is a place where the interests of environmentalists and millworkers coincide perfectly. In 1988, 4.3 billion board feet of logs were exported from U.S. ports on the Pacific coast – more than 25 percent of the total harvest from Oregon, Washington and Alaska. (Little was exported from California.) Although the logs shipped abroad do not come from federal land, the loss of logs from private and state land raises the pressure on the Forest Service and the Bureau of Land Management to cut more timber. It makes sense to try to get as much economic benefit as possible for the people who live around the forest, instead of exporting the logs and the jobs along with them.

Oregon, Alaska, California and Idaho tried to ban log exports but were rebuffed by the U.S. Supreme Court in 1984. Only the federal government can act, and only people like you can influence the government. Here's how:

• Write to Congress. Urge your senator and representative to allow states to decide whether to ban export of logs from private lands. (Your senator), U.S. Senate, Washington, DC 20510. (Your representative), House of Representatives, Washington, DC 20515.

• Write to the Department of Commerce. Secretary of Commerce Robert A. Mosbacher, Sr., Department of Commerce, 14th Street between Constitution and E streets, Washington, DC 20230.

Let's treat our forests right. A tremendous number of reforms are ripe to be made in the U.S. Forest Service, the Bureau of Land Management and the British Columbia Ministry of Forests. Your voice is crucial because public forests are the birthright of us all. You can ask that the agencies stop all cutting and road building in the ancient forests, and that timber sales elsewhere be reduced to levels that can be sustained without touching the precious remaining old growth. You might also suggest a small tax on lumber, with the proceeds to be directed to restoration projects that would employ more people in the forests. Besides writing to your legislators, the people who run the forest agencies need to hear your views.

• Write to your congressional representatives. Tell them that you care about saving the ancient forests, and ask them to support the establishment of an ancient forest reserve. (See addresses above.)

• Mail to the chiefs. The man in charge of the Forest Service is Chief F. Dale Robertson, Forest Service, Dept. of Agriculture, P.O. Box 96090, Washington, DC 20090. Also write to Director Cy Jamison, Bureau of Land Management, 1849 C Street, N.W., Washington, DC 20240.

• Home in on the ranger. In the United States, national forest-lands are divided into regions, the regions into forests, and the forests into ranger districts. In British Columbia, the divisions are regions and districts. You can direct your comments on particular agency actions or lands to the ranger of the relevant district, to the supervisor of that national forest, or to the regional forester responsible for that forest. Or you can just write to the regional forester to express your concern. The staff at the phone numbers listed can tell you how to get in touch with the officials in charge of specific forests or areas.

California: Regional Forester Ronald E. Stewart, 630 Sansome St., San Francisco, CA 94111. (415) 705-2870.

Washington and Oregon: Regional Forester John F. Butruille, 319 S.W. Pine St., P.O. Box 3623, Portland, OR 97208. (503) 326-3625. And: State Director D. Dean Bibles, Bureau of Land Management, 1300 N. E. 44th Ave., P. O. Box 2965, Portland, OR 97208-2965. (503) 280-7024.

British Columbia: Hon. Claude Richmond, Minister of Forests, 1450 Government St., Victoria, BC V8W 3E7, Canada. (604) 387-5255.

Alaska: Regional Forester Michael A. Barton, Federal Office Building, Box 21628, Juneau, AK 99802. (907) 586-8863.

A firm stand. It's in their own interests for the heads of lumber firms to be concerned about what their customers think. It was consumer communication that led tuna canners such as Star-Kist to refuse to buy tuna caught in ways that kill dolphins. Image is very important to corporate America. You might also let them know whether you would be willing to pay somewhat more for lumber if the funds were used for forest restoration to set right the problems created by past mismanagement. Write to these firms and let them know your suggestions and criticisms. If you think they're doing a good job, tell them. (You'll find their addresses in the next section.)

Seeing is believing

It's hard to get a feel for the forest just from reading a book or looking at pictures. Nothing can take the place of going to an ancient forest and seeing for yourself.

• Take a hike. Because most of the remnant ancient forests are on public lands, you don't need permission from anyone to see these treasures, just the transportation and sometimes a small entry fee. There are forests close to the road and others that require a full day's hike, to suit visitors of any athletic inclination. You can find these forests from slightly south of San Francisco, north along the California coast, through the Rogue River and the Kalmiopsis Wilderness of southwestern Oregon, to the lush rainforest of Washington's Olympic Peninsula and British Columbia's Vancouver Island. For the truly adventurous, the Tongass National Forest in the Alaska Panhandle probably offers the best chance for encounters with wildlife. (See list of addresses in the following section.)

• Keep an eye on your public lands. Equip yourself with a map, find out from rangers where logging has recently occurred and check it out. Let the people in charge know whether you like the job they're doing. It's as important to give forest agency managers positive feedback when they do well as to criticize them when they've acted irresponsibly.

• If there's a particular area you care about – one close to where you live or like to visit – monitor the timber activities there regularly. Federal agencies have to give notice to interested parties before they sell a tract of timber. If you make it known that you're interested, you can get notices of these proposals and comment on them. Check with environmental groups in your area to see what they think about these logging proposals. You can do the same for timber harvest on private land in California and Washington.

Spread the word

Now that you've learned something about ancient forests, the most important thing you can do is to keep the gift of knowledge moving. The more people come to know the ancient forests, the better our chance of preserving them for future generations. Here are a few ideas on how you can get more people involved.

• Talk to friends at your workplace, in your school, or to your family about the ancient forests. Tell them some of what you've learned in this book.

• Write to your local newspaper and express your opinion. Not only will this tell other readers about the issue, it will tell the editors of the paper that ancient forests are a topic their readership cares about, so they'll be more likely to cover the subject in more depth. Suggest that they start an environmental column, if they don't already have one. That way, you and your neighbors will be able to keep up on new developments.

• If you live in the West, speak to your child's teacher or scout leader about organizing a field trip to an ancient forest and volunteer to accompany the group. If you're in the East, travel to any forest for a demonstration. If you can't visit the forest in person, check out a video for an armchair journey to the Pacific Northwest. Either way, the learning experiences – in preparation as well as followup – can extend into all areas of study: reading, writing, map-making, history and mathematics as well as natural science. Write for The Wilderness Society's video and teacher's guide (For ordering information, see page 108).

• When you come back from a trip to the ancient forest, give a slide show for your friends, school, group or club. It's always more effective to see pictures and hear a story from someone you know than to simply see photos in a magazine.

• Pass along copies of this book and other materials on the ancient forests to friends, teachers and your local library.

• Celebrate the ancient forests in your community – in an art show, photo exhibit, poetry reading or essay contest at your local school, or even a costume party where people come as a creature of the ancient forest.

• Use your local schools in other ways. Help a teacher organize a unit on ancient forests, set up a panel discussion, help your kids put on a program on the ancient forests for a school assembly. Use Earth Day (April 22) and Arbor Day (April 27) as kickoffs and then keep the interest going by suggesting that your child's class "adopt a forest" to study throughout the year.

These are only a few possibilities. You can probably think of many more ideas.

Roots and connections

Plant a tree. Planting a tree is one of the best ways to reconnect with the forest. You don't have to plant an ancient-forest tree, either. Whatever forest is natural to your region will do fine. Find out what kinds of trees grow naturally in the place where you live. It makes sense to plant one of these native species, because you'll be introducing the tree into your local ecology. A native tree will strengthen the integrity of the ecosystem, while a non-native may disrupt it. Your local nursery, horticultural society, agricultural extension service or native plant society may be able to help provide you with information about the original trees of your area. If you live in a region where Douglas fir or ponderosa pine are native, you may even be able to plant a tree that also grows in the ancient forest. If you live in one of the few parts of the country where there are no native trees, you might consider setting aside a corner for whatever vegetation was native, such as prairie or desert scrub. Some groups can even arrange to have trees planted on your behalf if you are not able to plant one yourself. As an old proverb holds, "The best time to plant a tree was 20 years ago. The second-best time is now."

Support a group working on ancient forest issues. Each of us can only accomplish so much by ourselves. Some of the greatest advances in the protection of the environment have come about because of organizations that got together to lobby on behalf of all of us.

Each group working on the ancient forest issue has its own focus, which you can learn about by reading their publications at the library or by requesting that they send you information. Different groups have different tactics. Some work primarily through the courts, others through Congress and still others through public demonstrations, sit-ins and blockades. It pays to check them out before you join, so you can find one you feel comfortable with.

If you can spare a few dollars, even a small donation goes a long way in paying for the research and the campaigns to safeguard our ancient forests. You'll find a selection of these groups in the next chapter.

Learn more. You'll find lots of information about ancient forests in your local public library. In the next chapter, we recommend a few particularly good books that go into more depth about some parts of this issue.

Let us know what you think. At The Wilderness Society, we're always curious to hear your ideas. The more people are thinking about our forests' future, the better the chance that we'll come up with the best solutions. Send your comments and ideas to: The Wilderness Society, 900 17th Street, N.W., Washington, D.C. 20006, Attn: Saving Our Ancient Forests.

From Thought to Action

All of these methods, from letter writing to wood conservation, are needed to protect the ancient forests. Preserving them isn't something that can be accomplished by professionals alone. It requires the involvement of people like you who care about the forest and are willing to take action on its behalf.

Informing yourself on the fundamental issues, as you have by reading this book, is the first step. And you have not started

a moment too soon. Fortunately, some people have been working on behalf of the forests for more than a decade. Thanks to
them, there are still ancient forests to preserve. The next few
years will be crucial. Actions taken now will determine not
only whether there will be ancient forests for our children and
grandchildren to enjoy, but also whether there will be clean
water, clean air and a rich diversity of life to provide still
untold benefits to humanity for generations to come.

We stand at the point where two starkly contrasting futures
diverge. One is the bleak prospect of a depleted landscape with
mere fragments of ecologically impoverished forest remaining,
eroded hillsides, muddy streams and ghost towns. The other is
a much more hopeful vision: a region teeming with life, carpet-
ed with a diverse, healthy forest, providing habitats for a wide
variety of plant and animal species – an environment rich in
topsoil, clean air and flowing streams, as well as recreation and
jobs for people.

Your participation can make the difference in creating the
second scenario. Saving the ancient forests may seem like a big
order, and no one can do the job alone. Every effort helps,
even if you only write one letter. This book has given you the
essential tools you need to understand the ancient forests, the
threats they face and the opportunity to develop a better, more
informed relationship with them. The rest is up to you.

SIX

NATURAL
RESOURCES

NATURAL RESOURCES

Where to get additional information

Hopefully, this book has made you curious to find out more about our ancient forests and how you can help save them. These organizations can be a good starting point. They follow the issues and can help you stay up to date on the status of the forests and what needs to be done to protect them.

ORGANIZATIONS
National Groups

Association of Forest Service Employees for Environmental Ethics, P.O. Box 11615, Eugene, OR 97440. (503) 484-2692

Cooperative Extension (for help in selecting trees to plant in your area), affiliated with most county governments. Also called "agricultural extension."

Environmental Defense Fund, National Headquarters, 257 Park Ave. South, New York, NY 10010. (212) 505-2100

Regional Office: 5655 College Ave., Suite 304, Oakland, CA 94618. (415) 658-8008

Global ReLeaf, American Forestry Association, P.O. Box 2000, Washington, DC 20013

National Audubon Society, 801 Pennsylvania Ave. S.E., Washington, DC 20003. (202) 547-9009.

Oregon: Lane County Audubon, P. O. Box 5086, Eugene, OR 97405. (503) 485-2473

Washington: Seattle Audubon, 8028 35th Ave., N.E., Seattle, WA 98115. (206) 523-4483

National Wildlife Federation, 1400 Sixteenth St. N.W., Washington, DC 20036. (202) 797-6800

Natural Resources Defense Council, 40 West 20th St., New York, NY 10011. (212) 727-2700

Sierra Club, 730 Polk St., San Francisco, CA 94109. (415) 776-2211

Sierra Club Legal Defense Fund, 2044 Fillmore St., San Francisco, CA 94115. (415) 567-6100

The Wilderness Society, 900 17th St. N.W., Washington, DC 20006-2596. (202) 833-2300.

California: 116 New Montgomery, Suite 526, San Francisco, CA 94105. (415) 541-9144

Oregon: 610 S.W. Alder, Suite 915, Portland, OR 97205. (503) 248-0452

Washington: 1424 Fourth Ave., Suite 816, Seattle, WA 98101. (206) 624-6430

Southeast Alaska Natural Resources Center: 130 Seward St., Suite 407, Juneau, AK 99801. (907) 463-5333

Local and state groups

EPIC, P.O. Box 397, Garberville, CA 95440. Publishes a monthly environmental newsletter.

Friends of Opal Creek, P.O. Box 318, Mill City, OR 97360

Headwaters, P.O. Box 462, Ashland, OR 97520. (503) 482-4459

Klamath Forest Alliance, Box 577, Forks of Salmon, CA 96031. (916) 462-4742

Mendocino Environmental Center, 106 W. Stanley, Ukiah, CA 95482. (707) 468-1660

Native Forest Council, P.O. Box 2171, Eugene, OR 97402. (503) 688-2600

Northcoast Environmental Center, 879 Ninth St., Arcata, CA 95521. (707) 822-6918

Oregon Natural Resources Council, 1050 Yeon Building, 522 S.W. Fifth Ave., Portland, OR 97204. (503) 223-9001

Southeast Alaska Conservation Council, 419 Sixth Ave., Juneau, AK 99801. (907) 586-6942

Washington Environmental Council, 4516 University Way N.E., Seattle, WA 98105. (206) 547-2738

Western Canada Wilderness Committee, 20 Water St., Vancouver, BC V6B 1A4, Canada. (604) 683-8220

TIMBER COMPANIES

Here are some of the timber companies involved in logging the public forests of the Pacific Northwest. Do whatever you feel moved to do in good conscience to encourage them to cease this practice.

Top 10 purchasers of public timber in Washington and Oregon in 1989

(Ranked by Timber Data Company, Eugene, Oregon)

1   **Boise Cascade Corp.,** One Jefferson Square, Boise, ID 83728

2   **ITT Rayonier,** 1177 Summer St., Stamford, CT 06904

3   **Pacific Lumber & Shipping,** 3131 Rainier Bank Tower, Box 21785, Seattle, WA 98111

4 **Roseburg Forest Products Co.,** P.O. Box 1088, Roseburg,OR 97470

   Scott Pallets Inc., P.O. Box 657, Amelia, VA 23082

   Diamond Lumber, Inc., 190 Cohasset Road, Chico, CA 95926

5 **Hampton Affiliates,** Hampton Lumber Sales Co., 9400 S.W. Barnes Road, Portland, OR 97225

6 **Vanport Manufacturing,** P.O. Box 97, Boring, OR 97009

7 **Warm Springs Forest Products,** P.O. Box 810, Warm Springs, OR 97761

8 **WTD Industries, Inc.,** 10260 S.W. Greenburg Road, Suite 900, Portland, OR 97223

9 **Omak Wood Products,** 729 S. Jackson St., Omak, WA 98841

10 **Miller Shingle Company,** P.O. Box 29, Granite Falls, WA 98252

More public-timber purchasers

Bald Knob Land & Timber Company, 700 N.E. Multnomah, Suite 274, Portland, OR 97232

Bohemia Inc., 2280 Oakmont Way, P.O. Box 1819, Eugene, Oregon 97440

British Columbia Forest Products Ltd., 1050 W. Pender St., Vancouver, BC V6E 2X5, Canada

DAW Forest Products Co., 4000 Kruse Way Place, Bldg. 2, Suite 355, Lake Oswego, OR 97035

Eel River Sawmills, Inc., 1053 Northwestern Ave., Fortuna, CA 95540

Freres Lumber Company, Inc., P.O. Box 276, Lyons, OR 97358

Georgia-Pacific Corp., P.O. Box 105605, Atlanta, GA 30348

Johnson Group, P.O. Box 2314, Tacoma, WA 98401

Louisiana Pacific Corp., 111 S.W. Fifth Ave., Portland, OR 97204

MacMillan Bloedel Ltd., 1075 W. Georgia St., Vancouver, BC V6E 3R9, Canada

Malheur Lumber, West Highway 26, P.O. Box 160, John Day, OR 97845

Medco (Medford Corp.), P.O. Box 550, Medford, OR 97501

Ochoco Lumber, P.O. Box 668, Prineville, OR 97754

Plum Creek Timber Co., 999 Third Ave., Suite 2300, Seattle, WA 98104

Prairie Wood Products, P.O. Box 66, Riddle, OR 97469

Rogge Forest Products, Timber Products Sales, P.O. Box 269, Springfield, OR 97455

Sierra Pacific Industries, P. O. Box 4728, Redding, CA 96099

Simpson Timber Company, 1201 Third Ave., Seattle, WA 98101-3009

Sun Studs Inc., P.O. Box 1127, Roseburg, OR 97470

The Pacific Lumber Company, Box 37, Scotia, CA 95565

Weyerhauser Company, CH 1C28, Tacoma, WA 98477

Willamette Industries, P.O. Box 907, Albany, OR 97321

Wood Products Inc., P.O. Box 128, Oakland, MD 21550

CATALOGS, LISTS AND SUPPLIERS

Earth Care Paper Company, P.O. Box 3335, Madison, WI 53704. (608) 256-5522. Write for their catalog of recycled paper products.

Pacific Certified Ecological Forest Products, P.O. Box 1580, Redway, CA 95560. For a list of approved wood growers and suppliers, send a self-addressed, stamped envelope to PCEFP at the above address.

Northwest Botanicals, 1305 Vista Drive, Grants Pass, OR 97527. For a catalog of minor forest products and publications about them, send this company a self-addressed, stamped envelope.

Seventh Generation. (800) 465-1177. Publishes a catalog of environmentally sound household products and recycling equipment.

TJ International, 3210 East Amity Road, Boise, ID 83706. (208) 343-7771. This manufacturer of structural building materials and laminated wood windows was given a "Green Chip" award by *Family Circle* magazine for its contributions to the environment.

Wild Birds Unlimited, 1810 Broad Ripple Ave., Suite 8A, Indianapolis, IN 46220. Environmentally sensitive franchise company sells birdfeeders made only of non-old-growth wood.

FURTHER READING

Ancient Forests of the Pacific Northwest, Elliott A. Norse, The Wilderness Society/Island Press, 1990. Norse's detailed account covers the biology and values of the ancient forests and the ways in which they are endangered by logging and other threats.

The Earth Manual: How to Work on Wild Land Without Taming It, Malcom Margolin, Houghton Mifflin, 1975. Explains how to create wildlife habitat, plant trees, control erosion.

The Forest and the Trees: A Guide to Excellent Forestry, Gordon Robinson, Island Press, 1988. Robinson, forester for the Southern Pacific railroad for 27 years and since then the Sierra Club's chief forester, distills his experience into a handbook on how forestry ought to be practiced.

Forest Watch, monthly of Cascade Holistic Economic Consultants (founded by Randal O'Toole), with the most current thinking on forest issues. Includes *Reform!* a newsletter specifically devoted to restructuring the U.S. Forest Service. $21.95/year from CHEC, 14417 S.E. Laurie, Oak Grove, OR 97267.

For Earth's Sake: The Life and Times of David Brower, Gibbs Smith, 1990. Autobiography of an influential environmentalist.

Fragile Majesty, Keith Ervin, The Mountaineers, 1989. Ervin gives a journalistic account of the battle over timber in Oregon and Washington.

The Klamath Knot, David Rains Wallace, Sierra Club Books, 1983. Lyrical writing on the plants, animals and legends of the Siskiyou and Klamath mountains.

The Man Who Planted Trees, Jean Giono, Chelsea Green Publishing Co., 1985. The touching story of a country man who planted a forest of oak and beech trees in France.

Pacific Coast Tree Finder, Tom Watts, Nature Study Guild, 1973. Pocket-sized key to identifying Pacific Coast trees.

The Recycler's Handbook, Earth Works Press, 1990. More recycling ideas.

Reforming the Forest Service, Randal O'Toole, Island Press, 1988. A thorough analysis of the shortcomings of the agency that manages more ancient forest than any other.

Secrets of the Old Growth Forest, David Kelly and Garry Braasch, Peregrine Smith Books, 1988. Braasch's vivid color photographs and Kelly's text transport the reader into the ecology of the ancient forests.

The Simple Act of Planting a Tree: A Citizen Forester's Guide, Treepeople with Andy and Katie Lipkis, Jeremy P. Tarcher, Inc., 1990. A terrific hands-on manual based on Treepeople's extensive experience in Los Angeles.

Sometimes a Great Notion, Ken Kesey, Viking Press, 1964. Epic story of a logging family in western Oregon.

Tree Planning: A Guide to Public Involvement in Forest Stewardship, Joan E. Vance, British Columbia Public Interest

Advocacy Centre, 1990. Explains how the provincial forest-lands are managed and how to affect that process.

Tree Talk: The People and Politics of Timber, Ray Raphael, Island Press, 1981. Raphael's narration and Studs Terkel-style interviews give an honest picture of how people from a wide variety of perspectives view the forest.

Western Forests, Stephen Whitney, Audubon Society Nature Guides, 1985. For serious naturalists or weekend hikers who want to identify and understand what they see in the forest.

Working the Woods, Working the Sea, edited by Finn Wilcox and Jeremiah Gorsline, Empty Bowl Press, 1986. Stirring anthology of poetry, prose, photos and art on tree-planting, logging and salmon fishing in the Pacific Northwest.

GUIDEBOOKS

Exploring Oregon's Wild Areas, William L. Sullivan, The Mountaineers, 1988.

Hiking the Bigfoot Country: Exploring the Wild Land of Northern California and Southern Oregon, John Hart, Sierra Club Totebook, 1975. Consult more current maps to find recently designated wilderness areas and parks.

Visitors' Guide to Ancient Forests of Western Washington. By the Dittmar family for The Wilderness Society, 1989.

ESPECIALLY FOR KIDS

Children for the Green Earth, 307 N. 48th, Seattle, WA 98103. Sponsors a "Tree Planting Partnership," helping kids make contact with children in other countries who are interested in trees and the environment.

Children for Old Growth. P. O. Box 1090, Redway, CA 95560. Publishes an information-packed newsletter, poster for coloring other educational materials on old-growth forests and endangered animals.

Color the Ancient Forest. Living Planet Press, 1991. A kid's companion to *Saving Our Ancient Forests*, this 48-page coloring book features fun-to-color drawings of ancient forest plants and animals with interesting facts about them. Ages 4-8. To order, see item #102 on the last page.

The Lorax, Dr. Seuss, Random House, 1971. A classic parable of environmental destruction tinged with a glimmer of hope. (One logging equipment supplier tried – without success – to ban this book from his son's elementary school.)

Tree, David Burnie, Eyewitness Books, Alfred A. Knopf, 1988. Fine introduction to how a tree grows, reproduces and decays.

Trees: A Golden Guide, revised edition, Golden Books, 1987.

The Wild, Wild World of Ancient Forests. This 28-page teacher's guide and accompanying student activities sheet from The Wilderness Society is recomended for grades 4 through 6, but is adaptable for high-school use. Activities include reading tree rings, a predator/prey challenge and the staging of an environmental hearing. To order, see item #105 on the last page.

AUDIOVISUAL MATERIALS

Ancient Forests: Vanishing Legacy of the Pacific Northwest. This 13-minute color video from The Wilderness Society takes viewers into the heart of an ancient Douglas-fir forest and explores the intricacies of the ecosystem. It also discusses threats to the forest. Viewpoints from the U.S. Forest Service, the timber industry and the scientific and environmental communites are all represented. To order, send a check or money order for $19.95, plus $2.50 for shipping, to FilmComm, 641 North Ave., Glendale Heights, IL 60139; or call (708) 790-3300.

The Forest Through the Trees. Hour-long film on the battle over California's redwoods, shown on PBS. Available on videocassette for $40 plus tax and shipping from Green TV, 1125 Hayes St., San Francisco, CA 94117.

GLOSSARY

Algae: primitive, one-celled or multicellular plants that lack stems, roots and leaves, but usually contain chlorophyll.

Ancient forest: a forest that has undergone at least two centuries of natural succession. In the Pacific forests of North America, ancient forests are marked by trees of at least two species, including several large, living Douglas-fir or other coniferous trees that are at least 200 years old or more than 32 inches in diameter; a multi-layered canopy; standing dead trees; and large logs on land and in streams.

Bacteria: microscopic, single-celled organisms that break down the remains of other organisms.

Biodiversity: the variety of living organisms as seen on three levels: the variety of ecosystems, the variety of species, and the variety of genetic traits in organisms of each species.

Broadleaf: a flowering tree or shrub with relatively broad leaves, not needles or scales, and without woody cones like the conifers. (See *Hardwood*.)

Cambium layer: the layer of cells just below a tree's bark, which produces new wood and bark.

Canopy: the upper layers of a forest's trees, including branches and foliage, considered collectively.

Cant: a roughly cut, squared-off log.

Clearcutting: felling all the trees on a site in the process of logging it.

Conifer: a cone-bearing tree or shrub with needles or scales rather than broad leaves. (See *Softwood*.)

Deciduous tree: a tree that loses its leaves at the end of its growing season.

Decomposition: the process of decay that breaks down formerly living matter into smaller parts and chemical components.

Dormant: alive but inactive, with many biological processes slowed down or suspended.

Duff: the layer of organic debris on the forest floor – including fallen leaves, branches and animal droppings – and the organisms that decompose it.

Eastside forests: those forests occurring on the eastern side of the Cascade Range in Washington and Oregon, and of the Coast Range in Alaska and British Columbia.

Ecosystem: a community of living organisms in a particular area, their physical environment and the interactions among them.

Edge effect: the influence of a boundary between two types of habitat on the organisms that live near that boundary.

Fog drip: moisture that condenses onto the surface of vegetation and falls to the ground.

Fungus: a group of plant organisms that lack chlorophyll, reproduce through spores and often produce fruiting bodies, such as mushrooms or truffles. (See *Mycorrhizal fungus.*)

Gene: a unit of biological inheritance, passed on by an organism to its offspring, affecting these offspring's characteristics.

Greenhouse effect: the increase of carbon dioxide and certain other gases in the air, trapping heat near the earth's surface and preventing it from escaping into space, causing a rise in atmospheric temperature.

Habitat: the area or type of environment in which an organism or population normally lives.

Hardwood: the commercial wood of a broadleaf tree.

Invertebrate: an animal without a backbone.

Juvenile wood: wood formed in the innermost 15 or 20 rings at any given point on the tree.

Lichen: a type of plant composed of a fungus in close association with an algae.

Moss: a class of leafy, spore-bearing plants with thin stems and delicate leaf structures.

Mycorrhizal fungus: a type of fungus that forms a mutually beneficial association with a tree root, taking nourishment from it and providing other nutrients to the tree.

National forest: land owned by the American people and managed by the U.S. Forest Service.

Natural (native) forest: a forest of any age that arose without logging or planting.

New Forestry: an approach to forest management developed by university and U.S. Forest Service researchers that attempts to pattern logging after the size and severity of disturbances the forest experiences naturally.

Nurse log: a fallen log that supplies nutrients to the sprouts and seedlings of new trees that grow on it.

Old-growth forest: (See *Ancient forest.*)

Photosynthesis: the process by which green plants convert sunlight, water and carbon dioxide into new plant tissue and oxygen.

Saprophyte: a class of plants that do not photosynthesize, but rather draw their energy from the decay of organic matter.

Scat: animal droppings.

Seed tree cutting: a logging technique in which several live trees per acre are left behind to re-seed the logged area. The seed trees are cut once the seedlings become established.

Shelterwood cutting: a logging technique in which many live trees per acre are left standing to provide cover and partial shade. The older trees are cut once the younger trees become established.

Shrub: a woody plant or bush, smaller than a tree, with many stems rather than a single trunk.

Slash: organic debris left behind after a logging operation or other disturbance.

Snag: a standing dead tree.

Softwood: the commercial wood of a conifer tree.

Species: a group of actually or potentially interbreeding populations of plants or animals that cannot reproduce with other kinds of organisms.

Spotted owl: a species of owl, one subspecies of which (the northern spotted owl) makes its home in ancient forests and which was declared "threatened" in 1990 because of the decline in its habitat.

Springwood: wood produced early in the growing season, constituting the lighter part of the tree's annual rings.

Stand: a contiguous area of forest considered or managed as a unit.

Succession: the process, observed in wild ecosystems, in which the composition of plants and animals inhabiting a site changes over time.

Summerwood: wood formed near the end of the growing season, constituting the darker part of the tree's annual rings.

Sustainable forestry: a relationship between a human population and nearby forests in which the humans use forest resources at a rate and in a manner that can continue indefinitely without damage to the ecosystem.

Temperate forest: a forest that grows in the temperate zones, between the tropics and the polar regions.

Tree farm or **tree plantation:** a stand of trees planted and managed by humans primarily for timber harvest.

Truffle: a type of mycorrhizal fungus which grows underground in the soil.

Vertebrate: an animal with a backbone.

Virgin forest: an ancient forest that has never been logged or roaded.

Vole: a short-tailed rodent, otherwise resembling a rat or mouse.

Watershed: a region that drains its water into one body of water or river system.

Westside forests: forests on the western side of the Coast Range in Alaska and British Columbia, and the Cascades in Washington and Oregon.

INDEX

ABOUT THE AUTHOR

Seth Zuckerman is a widely published writer on environmental issues. His work has appeared in *Newsweek*, *The Nation*, *Sierra* and the *San Francisco Examiner*, among other publications. He holds an A.B. in energy studies at Stanford University and received an M.S. in energy and resources from the University of California at Berkeley. His graduate research addressed the social and ecological prospects for forestry after the exhaustion of old-growth forests. He has also taught ecology, environmental science, energy and mathematics. Zuckerman divides his time between the San Francisco Bay area and Humboldt County, California.

ABOUT THE WILDERNESS SOCIETY

Since 1935, The Wilderness Society has been the leading national conservation organization working to protect America's wild lands and wildlife. More than 90 million acres of wilderness have been permanently protected through the organization's efforts. The Wilderness Society's expert staff of scientists, lawyers, lobbyists and journalists work in the nation's capital and in 16 regional offices to safeguard America's legacy of natural resources. The group is supported by more than 400,000 members nationwide. In 1991, the Society's top priority is saving the ancient forests of the Pacific Northwest.

This book is made possible, in part, by a
generous grant to The Wilderness Society from
The Timberland Company

The Wilderness Society's
Ancient Forest Gifts

All proceeds support The Wilderness Society's campaign to save our ancient forests and other threatened wild lands.

> **The Wilderness Society membership.** You can become a member of The Wilderness Society with a contribution of only $15 or more. Please indicate your membership donation on the order form below.

Saving Our Ancient Forests. 128 pages; $5.95; **Item #101**

Color the Ancient Forest
> This delightful coloring book will introduce your children to the wonders of the ancient forests. Ages 4-8. 48 pages; $4.95; **Item #102**

Ancient Forest Tote bag
> Help save our forests by using this colorful and sturdy tote bag for carrying your groceries; 17"x12"x7"; $12.95; **Item #103**

Save Our Ancient Forests T-shirt
> Display your commitment to our ancient forests with this beautiful full-color 100% premium-cotton T-shirt. Available in small, medium, large and extra-large sizes; $14.95 each; **Items #104-S, 104-M, 104-L and 104-XL**

The Wild, Wild World of Ancient Forests
> Teacher's guide (See page 108 for description.); $3.00; **Item #105**

FREE with any purchase: Citizen's Action Kit
> (See page 90 for description and how to order separately.)

Ordering instructions

QTY	ITEM	UNIT PRICE	TOTAL
Maryland residents add 5% sales tax		$	
DONATION		$	
SHIPPING		$	
TOTAL		$	

Please make your check or money order payable to:
**The Wilderness Society,
P.O. Box 296,
Federalsburg, MD 21632-0296.**

Name: _____

Address: _____

Special discounts are available for bulk orders.
Call (202) 833-2300.

Please allow 6 to 8 weeks for delivery. Shipping and handling charges: for orders less than $15.00, include an additional $3.50; for orders $15.00 or more, include an additional $4.50.